AF553398

DANCE OF DEMOCRACY

By
Rajeshwar Prasad
Dept. of English
Sarvoday Post-Graduate College, Ghosi
Mau, (U.P.)
(India)

DISCOVERY PUBLISHING HOUSE PVT. LTD.
NEW DELHI-110 002

Published by:
Tilak Wasan

DISCOVERY PUBLISHING HOUSE PVT. LTD.
4383/4B, Ansari Road, Darya Ganj
New Delhi-110 002 (India)
Phone : +91-11-23279245, 43596064-65
Fax : +91-11-23253475
E-mail : parul.wasan@gmail.com
discoverypublishinghouse@gmail.com
web : www.discoverypublishinggroup.com

***First Edition:* 2013**

ISBN: 978-93-5056-248-2

Dance of Democracy

Printed at:
Dynamic Printers
Delhi

Dedicated to

Ram Bilas Singh,
My guru and guide,
Who made me;
Who taught me
To lead a life of virtue.

In the fiction, all the characters, places and events are fictitious. If there is any resemblance between these imaginary characters, places and events, it will be a mere coincidence.

Rajeshwar Prasad

Preface

There is democracy in many countries of the world. *Democracy is for the people, of the people and by the people.* Now the situation is that where there is no democracy the citizens of those countries raise demands for it. Law is supreme in it and it rules over the people. Humanity is supreme for all mankind and democracy works for the good of all mankind.

Democracy is flourishing all over the world in different ways. It is remarkable that where there is democracy, most of the people are satisfied with it and very few people demand the change in the governing system as in it the people get opportunity for their progress. In it none can deny the justice to the citizens and it establishes *equality based society*. Anyone can occupy the highest post according to the system established by law. Hence in it, there is no reign of a person but of law.

During the Indian Freedom Movement so many Indians sacrificed their lives in national interest—for the freedom of *Bharatmata*. They lost the sheer joy of their lives for the country. Some became widows. Some became widowers. Some became orphans. But now the situation is just opposite. None behaves well towards India. It seems that *Bharatmata* has no ability or capacity to give birth to such a son or daughter as was during the Indian Freedom Movement. None serves India but serves his or her own interest. The politicians as well as the common people ill-treat the country.

They do just opposite whatever they say on the stage. Democracy in India is treated differently. It has fallen into the hands of corrupt politicians. Indian politicians can be regarded as *democracy-charmers*. They deal it as they are magicians and behave as they are musicians. Sometimes some aspects of NC Chaudhuri's *Continent of Circe* come into my mind regarding India and the people of India. Getting such a critical situation of democracy in India, the largest democratic country in the world, I fear its future.

But finally I've firm faith and blind belief that the future of democracy in India is resplendent and also in all other countries of the world. I also believe that it will be able to do justice to everyone.

The problem is that English is not my own language and I can't say that it was the language of my fore-fathers. My mother tongue is *Magathi*....then Hindi. English is my second language. Many of us also think in English, express in English and write in English. The style is also a problem. We're Indians and we've English style infused into our expression . . . in Indian way. One has to present different ideas of a certain thought. Indeed it is a tale told by a person who has seen the situation of democracy in India carefully and pines for its betterment. It mustn't be forgotten . . . this is the country of Mahatma Gandhi.

Rajeshwar Prasad

Acknowledgements

Bachu Lal Singh, Rajnandan Prasad, Shyam Narayan Singh and Somnath Prasad, my tutors for their ispiring words and blessings.

Arbind Kumar Mishra, Sheo Shankar Bhagat, Shreesh Tripathi, Rajendra Yadav and Rajani Kumari for their inspiration and sympathy.

Sanyukta Kumari, my wife for her great but unseen contribution to the creation of this work of art.

Tilak Wasan, the Director and the editorial staff of Discovery Publishing House Pvt Ltd for taking keen interest to publish this book. Without Tilak Wasan's keen interest to publish it at proper time, this book wouldn't have been this book.

And finally but immensely, my elder brothers Rameshwar Prasad and Dashrath Prasad for their love and support.

Thank you.

Contents

Preface

Acknowledgements

1. Birth and Happiness ... 1
2. Achievements ... 9
3. Works of Welfare ... 18
4. Pillage and the A^+ University ... 25
5. Assembly Election ... 30
6. Coronation of the Limcaman ... 38
7. Right to Information ... 48
8. Religion for Scandal ... 53
9. Election for only Stability ... 60
10. Home Ministry and Red Light Men ... 70
11. The Top Secret Meeting ... 76
12. The Samadhan Commission ... 83
13. The Election ... 96
14. The Sword on Corruption ... 104
15. Law is Supreme in Democracy ... 116
16. Sitaram and His Realization ... 120

Notes ... 127

Index ... 135

1

CHAPTER

Birth and Happiness

There was happiness and happiness—only happiness. None was unhappy. Each one was in the lap of divine bliss. Narayan has got a baby only six days ago. He was very happy and sat on a kingly chair made of sedge. Different kinds of sweets were got made to distribute among the people on the occasion of *chhathhi*.

It was Saturday. A large number of people were assembled there to participate in the celebration. The newly born baby lay on a bed. The bed was in the middle part of the court of Narayan's house. Sona, Narayan's wife was also sitting on the same bed on which the baby was lain. In the meantime, the baby was crying. The people said that the child was extra-ordinary because of his particular type of voice. They also said that Sona and Narayan were very fortunate, who had given birth to such a baby. They said that he will redeem not only his family but also the whole country.

"...he is another Rama. He will redeem his family—his village—our country and the world, too. He will be the determiner of us—of the world, and will redeem mother India from, bribery, prostitution, rape, robbery, commissionism, racialism, casteism, communism... There will be no evil on earth. The earth will become Paradise as was the Garden of Eden. There will be an overwhelming current of love and brotherhood all over the world. He will launch a mission of cosmopolitanism," said the people present there.

Listening to all this Narayan said emotionally, "He will redeem the whole world. There will be no evil on earth. I'll do everything possible for his bright career—for the world's bright career...."

In the blissful and optimistic atmosphere, the rituals of *chhathhi* began. The baby was bathed along with his mother. Many women were assembled there, too, who participated in the rituals. Many types of sweets were distributed among the people. Eating sweets they were very happy. They claimed, "Its taste is not like ordinary taste of sweets. Its taste is like manna. Its taste is mysterious...." They were very happy to know that the baby will not only redeem them, but also the world and they began to wait impatiently for the TIME, when they will be redeemed by the very person. Their basic attitude was changed and were very hopeful about their redemption.

Narayan was very cautious for his son's resplendent future. He decided to provide everything which was suggested by the priest. He also desired to name his son according to the horoscope prepared by the priest.

Therefore, he went to Kapilmuni to get the horoscope made. He had also carried 11 kgs rice, 2.5 kgs pulse, 2.5 kgs potato, 250 gms salt, 250 gms turmeric, some spices through his servant along with Rs. 1001 to donate Kapilmuni as a *dakshina.*

As Kapilmuni saw all this, he became very happy. He told Narayan to sit on a holy mat, while he sat on a chair made of sedge having worn maroon garments with Sitaram... Sitaram... Sitaram... print. He had long-grey beard.

Things were kept on a plank. Narayan sat on the mat. Kapilmuni said to him to wait for some minutes and began to comb his long hairs and beard, which took only thirty minutes.

After arranging his hair, he said to Narayan, "Tell me Narayan. Tell me. What's the matter? You're very lucky. Hence you have come here now; otherwise I was just to leave my home to participate in the holy chant of the *Ramayana.* Tell me soon. I'm already too late...."

Hearing him, Narayan narrated the story of his baby's birth in detail. He also told him about the mysterious cry or voice of the baby and the people's expression.

Listening to him, Kapilmuni, his religious priest took out his almanac from his red wallet and began to turn the pages of the almanac. Later he asked, "What is the date of birth of the baby? When was he born? Where was he born? What is the name of his mother?"

"It was Saturday... 25th of February, 1967. He was born at 7.30 AM. He was born at the verandah in my *kothhi* of Bharatpur. The name of his mother is Sona," said Narayan.

Kapilmuni continued to turn the pages of the almanac for quarter minutes and said, "... you're King Dashrath... Sona is Queen Kaushlya. The baby is Lord Rama—he is an incarnation of God. He is born from the womb of Sona to abolish all the evils on earth. The earth will be turned as Paradise—another Paradise—the Paradise on earth. He will redeem the whole world from the worldly sins. There will be *Ram-Rajya* not only in India but all over the world. The deer and the lion will live together—will eat together—will drink together. There will be an atmosphere of love and brotherhood not only in the human society but also in the society of the animals. Lions will live in our houses with our cows, oxen, buffalloes, goats, calves... without any kind of fear and terror. Man will feel no fear to go near lions, tigers and other wild animals...."

"... but O Narayan! There is also a great danger to his life. So you must have to save him from air, fire and water until five years of his age. If he remains alive for five years in your lap, none on earth will harm him—defeat him...," he continued.

After some moments he said again, "One thing is also very remarkable for you—for his life—for his successful life, you will have must to celebrate a priest-feast of 1001 Brahmins. On the occasion you should donate 1.25 *paseries* gold, 1.25 hectares of land, 1.25 quintals rice, 1.25 hundred metres red cloth, 1.25 mounds pulse, 1.25 *paseries* turmeric... to the Brahmins."

As Narayan heard that he had to donate 1.25 *paseries* gold, he began to see up and down. He kept silent for some minutes.

Meanwhile Kapilmuni was looking at his face as the hunter looks at the prey. Later Narayan dared to speak and said, "but... but... but... but... O Baba! I'm able to donate all the things said by you but not gold. I'm ready to donate 1.25 *paseries* brass instead of gold as it is also yellow like gold."

Kapilmuni said, "O Raja Dashrath! The great king like Raja Dashrath! Muster courage and zeal. You must not forget, you're a king like King Dashrath who has given birth to a redeemer of all mankind from the worldly evils. Are you not getting? Only due to your only baby your name will be skyrocketted. You will shine as the sun and will enlighten the whole world. You must not forget the day when the whole world will be under your light—under your feet. You will smile in the sky. You must try to do everything possible to perform the priest-feast. You've enough land. You're one of the well-known jemindars of India. You may sell some *riyasats* to perform the feast...."

Narayan said, "O Baba! If you say, I'll do this anyhow, because this is the matter of my baby's life—of my own life—of my future. This will change our fate. One day I'll definitely shine as the sun shines. I'll enlighten the world and the world will be under my feet. I'll smile in the sky and the world will see my smile. I'll be the Divine Light. If you say. If you say, I've no hesitation to sell the *riyasat* of the Kunda Estate. *Lost the Kunda Estate; Gained the whole world*. I'm sure! Definitely! None on earth can prevent me—can prevent my son—can prevent the redeemer of the world...."

Meanwhile Kapilmuni was nodding and smiling. He said, "Now you understood everything. I think I need not to say anything more. I told you everything but only because of you otherwise...."

Narayan said, "Yes! Yes! I get it Baba !I get it! Tell me the proper name of my baby according to the almanac."

"The proper name is just before you," Kapilmuni replied.

"Where?"

"You don't see! Just before your eyes on the garments of the Baba —your respected Baba."

"Oh! I'm sorry! I'm too sorry Baba! Too sorry! Sitaram!"

"Yes! Yes! Right you're... Sitaram... only Sitaram...."

This is only proper name of your lovely baby according to my almanac. I examined and calculated my all the almanacs... new and old... the *Thakur Prasad* & others, came to the conclusion that the proper name of your son should be 'Sitaram'. Half of King Janak... half of King Dashrath... half of Janakpur and half of Ayodhya... half of the goddess... half of the god... half for the sky... half for the earth... fifty-fifty...."

Narayan was listening to all this very carefully. He became very glad. He stood up and said very gloriously, "If Baba says I'll sell not only Kunda Estate but some other estates, too, if necessary. Saying *'I salute you'* and touching his holy feet, he went his home.

After three months Narayan celebrated the priest-feast with great pomp and show. In it 1001 Brahmins participated. He provided all the things suggested by Kapilmuni.

The Brahmins celebrated *joyful life rituals* before the beginning of the feast. Sitaram sat on a mat made of *kush.* Kapilmuni spread holy water on his body, pasted sandal-wood paste into his forehead with his ring figure and chanted holy hymns in Samskrit.

In the meantime Sitaram began to smile and when holy water was spread on his body he felt restless. Seeing it Kapilmuni spoke, "It is obvious... quite obvious. Undoubtedly he will redeem the whole world from evils. His smile is divine—and indicates what not! His hands are very long which indicate that *He* is one of the incarnations of God... 25th incarnation... Aha! Aha! 25th incarnation of God in your lap."

After the celebration, Kapilmuni came out of the house of Narayan to depart from there, meanwhile Bhageran, who was a hay-trusser came to him and said, "O Baba! Baba ! Dukhani, my wife has given birth to a child. He is my eleventh child and the first son. He is very robust. Please tell me about his future and a proper name for him. Almighty God has awarded me a son after the daughters. He is my life... my breath... my pulse... my everything."

"I know him. I know it completely. You're very lucky. He is the light of your house. He will be a great grazer and will graze alone all the cattle of the whole village. He 'll earn and you'll enjoy. You're Bhageran! No ! And he is Khaderan; therefore No! Khaderan ! Bhageran's son Khaderan! What a suitable name! What a good match, What a good name for your son! How! You should give him the milk of a strong pig, so that he could become strong and robust, because after you he'll have to fulfil all of your requirements— all the requirements as a grazer of the village. I've firm faith and blind belief, he'll be able to perform your duties—duty to graze the cattle successfully, because this is the tradition of your family. Tageran... Haregan... Sidhegan... Phulegan... Paregan... Bhageran... Khaderan... Aha! Seven generations! Yes seven generations ! There is enough chance! He'll be...,"said Kapilmuni.

Bhageran said to him, "But... O Baba ! I want to get him taught. Six generations of my family passed. They grazed cattle, but only the salt-bread was availabl. Now...is and will be available. I want, the baby of the seventh generation should be the *determiner*... not the grazer, who'll determine the fate of our country because nowadays none is safe... none gets justice... the poor and the gentle men are suppressed and considered fool and mad—and the dishonest men and the rich are considered as men... as honest... as true.... *Might is right* everywhere in India. I want its abolition by my son... by my own son... at any cost."

Kapilmuni replied, "Are you mad? Bhageran? Do you not know your traditional profession is very very risk free and very very pleasant...? While grazing the cattle in the field, from where you can enjoy charms and beauty of Nature. Indeed you are a poet. You're Wordsworth... a poet of Nature. Your body is automatically exercised... best; for your Khaderan, too. You can feel yourself... you're very healthy... but I'm lean and thin. You're free... quite free. There is no problem of paper and pen... notebook... and book... dress and table... art and science... grammar and translation... school and college. No risk... no responsibility. Indeed you are a great man. Do you know that engineers, doctors, teachers, politicians, scientists, lawyers... work night and day but you only during the day. They waste their minds... their bodies... their health. Their jobs are full of risk. They are overloaded with responsibilities but you're not less than a king... a king of the meadows... no risk... no responsibility. Now you can imagine your place, your risk free profession. You shouldn't think anything more. You shouldn't leave your traditional job. If you leave it... it will be a great mistake of your life. Do you understand all this Bhageran?"

"But O Baba! Time is changed. Here there is democracy... the rule of law... one can hold higher to highest post. His proper name is Deshraj, no Khaderan. He will change the future of the country. He'll abolish corruption from the country. There will be no exploitation, no suppression, no atrocity, no anarchy—everywhere an atmosphere of love and brotherhood... all round development of the country. I'll get him taught at any cost and will apply the *do and die* policy for his resplendent future. I know its formula... *the diligence is the key to success.* No diligence; no success. The fulfilment of duties is the *aid* of success. So, O Baba! Please, bless my son to reach the highest post...."

Kapilmuni said, "My blessing is with you and your son but you mustn't forget what you're."

CHAPTER

Achievements

Sitaram was admitted to most of the reputed private schools, run by the well-known scholars for his primary and high school education. In a year at least 2-3 schools were changed. In this kingly process he was taught in more than hundred schools. Thousands of the private tutors also taught him at his home. Narayan continued to say to the tutors not to say any word for doing anything wrong, because he was a redeemer of the world. The teachers of the schools had also to follow his advice. Therefore, the tutors behave and teach him very cautiously so that he could pass the target of one month, because Narayan had declared that the tutor able to teach him for full a month, he would be given one kilogram gold and hundred acres of land. To get this reward, they tried to do the best of their knowledge and capacity but none could pass that tough examination and most of them were changed and dismissed.

With and within this long process of changing the schools and the private tutors he passed Intermediate of Arts Examination and was placed in the third division.

Passing the Intermediate of Arts Examination, he was admitted to Model University, Kashi. It was situated in a very big city. Kashi was regarded as the most old and holy city of the country. Sitaram decided to enjoy the charm of the city. For the fulfilment of the motive he decided to collect donation on the occasion of Holi, a well-known and important festival of the Hindus; and enjoyed the festival with great pomp and show. People said that such a pompous programme of the Holi festival was never celebrated in Kashi. Knowing this his father was very happy. He said, *"Mahabodhi of Sitaram."*

That was not the last *bodhi*, but after that a number of such *bodhies* had been obtained by Sitaram on other occasions like; *Dushehra, Deepawali, Srikrishnajanmasthami, Shivaratri* etc. On such occasions, he with his friends and like-minded people made barricades on the roads of the city and continued to collect money from passers by, vehicle drivers etc forcibly. They did the same with the shopkeepers of the city. If anyone failed to pay, he was badly beaten by them. The police also failed to protect the common people from barbarism and atrocity of Sitaram and his supporters.

Collecting the donation, he celebrated the festival with great pomp and show. He also called some lady dancers like; Sonabai, Phulbai, Amarbai and Rajanigandha to dance on such occasions. He also got a suit made on the occasions and anyhow he saved heavy amount from the amount of donation. His friends were also lucky like him and they also took advantages on such occasions.

As the festivals had to begin they went to the lodges of the city in which the students live to collect donation and they were forced to pay donation. If anyone who failed to do so they were badly beaten. Some were also killed each year and none could know the fact that who killed them. Who were poor and unable to pay donation to them left their lodges during the period of the celebrations.

At least one person was definitely killed each year by Sitaram and his friends in the Donation Collection Movement. But the police regarded that that was an accident. His father was very happy and satisfied with his performances in Kashi.

Listening to the glory of Sitaram his father said, "Aha! Aha! My loveliest! Aha! He is not an ordinary man but indeed an incarnation of God—25th incarnation. He is the son... and son like him has to none...."

One day it happened that Sitaram and his friends were collecting donation on the main road from the vehicle drivers. His friends also stood on the road to stop the vehicles. Meanwhile a truck came. Seeing that they stood in the middle of the road and indicated the driver to stop the truck. They also showed him a volume of the tickets. But the driver didn't stop the truck and crushed all the nine students. Crushing them the driver with the truck fled away and they died on the spot.

But Sitaram was such an incarnation that not even a single drop of tear came out from his eyes. He stood still and looked like a philosopher fallen into thinking.

After some minutes he spoke, "They are too... mis... for... tu... nate. This year is very much advantageous. By the last of the year they would have become men of lacs. But let them die. It was written in their fate. It was bad luck, otherwise all of them would have purchased *Ambassadors* like me this year. But I'm very much lucky. God has saved my life. It is a great lesson to me. From the next day none will stand on the road. I will get a big stone kept on the road to stop the vehichles. They, therefore, will automatically stop here. There will be no problem. The police will not disturb me—and can't disturb us. What will they do? They will also share my collection. No more than this. They will take only small part of my collection. They are in the government service to earn not to maintain law and order, if they try to do so—try to maintain law and order, they will be themselves swallowed by it. This is free India, where everything is possible by those who are mighty, influential, and wealthy...."

Meanwhile people were nodding and saying "Yes... yes... yes...."They were happy, too.

Listening to him they said, "He is another Shiva of the city... another... who will definitely redeem the humanity from the worldly evils. Aha! Aha! Our redeemer!"

The next morning he went to a private coaching centre of the city, which was run by Prof Gautam, and demanded Rs. 50051. He also gave a receipt to him saying, "Give me, soon. I have also to go to others. I'm too busy. It is Durga Puja, tomorrow."

"Take Rs. 1001 only."

"This? Alm? What is this... ?

"Please get it. I've to pay it to you from time to time."

Getting Rs. 1001, Sitaram said, "Try to give more and more as possible on the occasion of this great festival of Hindus. Are you not a Hindu... ?

"It is enough. I've also to give it to some others, who continue to come here."

"O Gautam! don't try to show himself a philosopher. Don't deliver philosophy before me. Give sufficient amount... otherwise...."

"O my disciple! My dear disciple! Dearest! At present I'm quite unable to give such a heavy amount."

"Listen to me very carefully. Care... fully. You've to give or not to give. Do you want to go to hell? Do you know what is hell? Hell...?"

"As you know I give money to you each year on each occasion. Now I lack. Later I'll try to pay more and more."

"O Gautamaa- Fautamaa! Cunning Gautama! Don't bargain with me, else the result will be tragic for you. You've to give me Rs. 50051 or will have to go into abyss. Do you get it?"

Knowing it Prof. Gautam gave him Rs. 10000 and said, "O my dearest disciple... now, go away."

But Sitaram became furious. Threw all the rupees to his body and slapped more than four times.

Slapping he said, "You'll not see the next sun."

It was night. At midnight an ambulance in which there was a patient came to the Government Hospital, Kashi for treatment. Dr Naresh, who was Prof Gautam's younger brother, was on emergency duty at that very night. The patient was floundering and was expressing too much pain in abdomen. Dr Naresh began his treatment. In the meantime he was kidnapped and was brought to his home by the persons who had gone with the patient. He was said by them to get the door opened. But he denied to do so at any cost. He, therefore, was beaten too much by them at the door. When they were beating him he was crying, "Don't open the door at any cost."

They, therefore, became more violent and cut his right hand, and threw it to the house through a peep hole. Prof Gautam was listening to his cry and as he saw the hand, he couldn't remain in the house and came out of the house to save the life of his brother.

As he came out, he was gunned down. He fell into the ground and said, "Kill me... not my brother."

Saying it he slept a sleep, which knew no waking.

Killing him they fled away. None could know who killed him because none reached there when Dr. Naresh was crying.

Three years passed. Sitaram continued to do the same. He passed the BA Examination and was placed in the first class first. He was awarded a gold medal for his performance in the examination. Knowing it Narayan became very happy and his happiness was easily seen in his dialogue, eating, food, lodging, clothing etc.

Getting it Narayan said, "O Si... ta... ra... m you've done an uphill task. Others of my area kill time... and you... a gold medallist... first class first."

Getting the award Sitaram went home. He was welcomed as a prophet... as a messiah.

Seeing him Narayan said, "Come! Come! My dearest come! Come here the gold medallist. How did you work so that you got first class first. You'll be a prosperous ruler like King Augustus... like Solomon...."

He continued, "Tell me. How do you work? I know you'll have worked hard. You'll have expended your mind and heart too much."

"Respected father! I'm not such a son who works and then gains something. Know it. I'm not such a man who works hard and gains first position in the examination. Is there any examiner, who can avoid my desire. If anyone who does so he will be thrown into abyss—will go to hell. Had or has anyone courage to do so. None! None can ignore my order," said Sitaram.

He continued, "Now you can imagine my might. I swallowed a number of persons like gram but none could harm me. Have you listened to the name of Prof Gautam, who was a reputed professor of the university? Do you? No? Know. He went into hell. None speaks before me. I've bought a large apartment in Kashi which costed Rs 90 lac. For the purpose, I took not even a single pice from you. It is the most *hi-fi* and latest model building in Kashi. Rs. 35 lac is balance in my accounts. I've also bought an *Ambassador* car and a *Marshal*. When I pass in the streets—on the roads, each person looks at me."

"You're great. Indeed. None in the world can take your place. I'll plant a banyan tree in your name," said Narayan.

Sitaram said, "I'll skyrocket your name. Your name will be written even in water."

"... Indeed your achievements are imitable. Man should follow you— follow your path. You're a pathfinder. Are you getting all this? A pathfinder! Khaderan is too mean and corrupt—is too foolish—is too dull. He is two months younger than you. He has also passed BA Examination, but was placed in the second division. In the second division! Do you know?

What is his name on the records? Deshraj! His father's name is Bhageran and his son's name Deshraj. Bhageran grazes cattle. Grazer's son—Deshraj. If he'll be light, who will be dark? He should graze cattle. It is better for him. If he reads in the university, who'll graze the cattle in the village. He passed in the second division. What is the use of the second division degree in this age of competition? He is killing his valuable time. He should follow the prophecy of Baba—of Kapilmuni. But he is trying to change the platform of his life. Is it possible? It is never possible. At last he'll repent," said Narayan.

"Yes... yes... yes!"

Sitaram stayed with his father in his paternal home and after fifteen days he left his home for Kashi. He was admitted to the same university to do MA in Political Science; and got a cut-out hung on the main gate : *'Sitaram, the next candidate and the best candidate.'*

He continued to sit there to touch the feet of professors of the university, to shake hands with the male students and to say *'namaskar bahinji'* to the female students. This hard work continued for a long period. Sometimes he had to fall on the feet of the students—especially of the male students not of the female students, after a long period of two and a half months, the polling for the *Students Union Election* was held on 30th September.

For the election he seized eighty-nine cars and jeeps forcibly, but neither the police nor the public did anything against him. He also got the support of an influential political party. He collected a heavy amount of donation from the shopkeepers and the vehicle drivers forcibly.

The students had also to pay donation to him for the democratic festival. None had courage to deny to do so. Each person had to pay donation as per demand of Sitaram. After the election Rs. 23 lac was balance in his accounts.

Each wall and board of the university was covered with his posters. Big posters were pasted even into the office board of DC, Kashi. The university board was also covered with posters and election slogans:

Sitaram is the best;
'Our great glory.'

Sitaram is the best;
'Others are worst.'

Vote for Sitaram;
'For others shoes and sandals'

Sitaram is a redeemer;
'All corruption cleaner.'

There was also a huge photograph of Sarvoday Singh, a political leader on each poster of Sitaram's election campaign with a motto at bottom: *'A symbol of sacrifice and martyr'*. It was written at the bottom of the photograph of Sitaram: *'A Messiah: A redeemer.'*

On the date of the polling the security arrangement was tightened. It seemed that the university was an army cantonment. Wine and food was available free of cost. There was a huge tent near the main gate of the university from where his supporters were chanting slogans:

Sitaram is the best,
All others are dust.
Winning he'll redeem,
And will launch a scheme.
Son of the university,
Like God and deity.

Each has to vote for him
Or has to get them
Shoe, sandal and clap
With a full warm slap.

Losing they will go
Winning they'll gain
Many bullets of 351
And none will be saved.

A K 47 is before them,
Sitaram is before them
They'll have to choose—
Will they have to lose?

Amidst the slogans the polling was being continued. His supporters were eating and enjoying. Meanwhile, all of his supporters were away from the vegetarian food.

By 4 PM the polling process was finished and after six hours the result was declared. Sitaram was declared victorious. Himanshu, who was his rival could get only one per cent vote.

The next day, a victory procession was begun from his election office. Thousands of students and some others also participated in the procession. There was a band of musicians with them. Sitaram was sitting in a chariot type open jeep, which was decorated with the latest items. The whole crowd was following it and was moving forward very slowly.

Most of the sweet vendors had closed their shops. But whenever and where'er they got sweet shops they entered the shops and ate all the sweets without paying price. They also broke locks of the closed sweet shops. The same was the situation of the wine-shops and none had courage to object them. The police were enjoying instead of watching. They were intoxicated. But where was Himanshu, none could know. The dancers along with the students were dancing blissfully to the tone of hit film songs. The people of both sides of the streets and the road were enjoying from their own doors and roofs. The main road was jammed for six hours. Meanwhile an ambulance carrying two patients in critical condition came. The relatives of the patients requested them to leave the way but none gave the way to it to pass by the road. Therefore, both the patients died there. But not even a single ray of shame came to their faces... not even a single drop of tear came out from their eyes. The procession remained continued for the whole day.

Works of Welfare

Sitaram began to perform his work—work of welfare in the university. He continued to sit in the office and promised the students of the university to abolish the corruption of the university.

In his own office, there was a name-plate but the particular type of name-plate: *'Sitaram: A corruption cleaner'*. Seeing it the students smiled and said, "He'll definitely win laurels. He is a handsome man—a polar star."

After a month he made his contact with Prof Suraj who was the proctor and said to him to provide a couple of suits and shoes for him, if he desired to remain tension free for the session. Firstly he denied to do so, but later he gave all that to him.

Getting it Sitaram said, "Now none can harm you. You're free—free to do everything."

"Thank you so much Sitaram. Now let me do everything possible. I'll never disturb you. You're also free," said Prof. Suraj.

Prof. Suraj usually continued to go to the department once in a week or in two weeks by car and sat in the office. He continued to hold his classes rarely and when the students requested him to hold classes for them, he replied very sweetly, "Do you not know that diamond is not found everywhere. Diamond is not everywhere. Are you getting me? Mirza Ghalib... Romila Thapar... are not everywhere. I'd topped MA in BHU. I'm not an ordinary professor like others. Therefore my physical presence in the class is not necessary – my symbolic presence in the class routine is enough. But I promise you, at least one class will be held by me before the final examination. Don't worry. You're very lucky...."

Prof. Suraj knew the new way of walk. His residence was only three kilometres away from the university and there was a stadium in the university. He usually continue to go to the stadium and moved round 15-20 times by the car saying that he enjoys fresh wind through the window of the car. And after some minutes he went back to his residence.

Usually he continued to go to the office at 10 AM and sat in the chamber for some minutes. After this he visited the officers of the university and talked about several issues of the university. In his discussion one thing was very important that he was never rigid to any point, because he had to adjust to each one.

Whatever words came from his mouth was sweet like *manna*. For the purpose he usually spoke, "Yes it happens. It may happen. Let it go."

While speaking he smiled very much. Seeing anyone he smiled firstly.

In his daily life he had discovered a maxim: *'misappropriate and let misappropriate'*. For this maxim he was very popularly known. He usually continued to say, *"If anyone desires to live in peace and rest he or she should be practical.* He should follow whatever is said by the masses. He or she must misappropriate and let others misappropriate."

The theory of good adjustment was properly fulfilled by him. In 25 years of service as a Superintendent of Sports any investigation agency or any auditor didn't object his financial operation, rather he was fully praised by them. He was regarded as a great man of *Adjustment*. Some persons said, "He is *Narad.*"

The auditors were very much satisfied with him. They also praised him too much. They said, "He is a very honest man who himself distributes the amount—the holy amount. He himself gives us fifty per cent amount of the bills. We have never seen any honest man like him in our lives. This is why, he is free—quite tension free, otherwise there are a number of superintendents like him, who claim to be honest and don't give even a single pice to us. Therefore, there are so many objections against them."

There were two groups (unauthorized) of the employees in the university. They praise their own groups. But Prof Suraj was a unique person. It was not very easy to say that in which group he belonged to—which type of person he was, because he always tried to maintain his balance in both groups. He remained in contact with them so that he could get the maximum advantage. Only one per cent of the staff said that he was the slave of advantage—a great sucker of advantage. But ninety-nine per cent people were too much happy with him.

Some students claimed that there was misappropriation in the university library. Therefore Sitaram picketed the university library. In the beginning, the university administration was ready to give rupees one lac secretly to stop picketing, but he demanded rupees two lac. Finally, the administration became ready to appoint a committee to investigate the library expenditure in which Sitaram was a member.

The enquiry began which passed for five days. After five days, the committee submitted its report, "... There are many books in the library index, but they are not available in the library or have not been issued to anyone. There are many books which have been mentioned waste on the records but after binding, the same books have been mentioned as newly purchased books. There are many books into which the price-stickers are pasted which show higher price than the actual price. There are some book receipts but the books are not available in the library. Some books are quite useless in the library which have been purchased by the authority to expend money so that they could get maximum commission...."

The committee found the defalcation of rupees eighty-seven lac during the period of last five years. Knowing it, the committee wondered and the report was submitted to the university administration. It recommended to take necessary action against the library authority. But Ramanna, Vice-Chancellor refused to do so and said that all the issues of the library had already been investigated eight times but no irregularity was found in the past. Sitaram was against the view of the vice-chancellor and decided to oppose his decision.

One new issue came to light in the university, Mataram, Sitaram's friend was performing practical work in the laboratory of Geography. By chance, a clock fell down from his hand and broke up. Therefore, Prof Mercy, who was the head of the department penalized him. He ordered him to pay fine of Rs. 800 only but he denied to do so. There was a tussle between Sitaram and Prof Mercy, too. Many students assembled near the gate and Sitaram addressed them, "... lacs of rupees of the practical fee of the students are misappropriated by Prof Mercy and some others each year. The professor and the principal take shoes, inverter, refrigerator, TV, CD player, clothes, etc. in commission—as bribe. The suit which Prof Mercy has worn today is given by a supplier. I know it, who has given him an *Aqua-Guard*, a water filter. Some other professors have got laptops. They prepare bogus records of an auction of the old equipment of the laboratory and is mentioned waste and broken. But the fact is that the same old equipments is mentioned as newly purchased equipment on the stock registers. So, Mataram or any other will not pay any kind of fine in future. I promise before you that I'll disclose all the issues before media...."

Getting it, Prof Mercy dismissed his own order of collecting fine from Mataram. He met Sitaram at home and requested him, not to raise the issue. At his home Prof Mercy was in need of *mercy* of Sitaram and said very pathetically, "... O Sitaram! O Babu! Sitaram Babu! I'm your *guru*—your tutor. Do you not know—*Guru gurúve bhawah.* The teacher is God. I, therefore, am God—not less than God. Please get this holy envelope and speak nothing. Mind that I'm your esteemed *guru*...."

Taking the envelope, Sitaram said, "... ex... cu... se... me.... I'm with you. I'm for you. Even at midnight I can do anything for you. During the heavy rain, too. I'll speak nothing. I'll not disclose it to media. Let it go."

Only one month had passed that one another issue came to light in the university. The building which cost rupees eighty lac and was finished in September, inaugurated in October, collapsed on 1st November. In it eighty-one students died. Therefore, *The End of the Corruption Movement* began in the university. Sitaram was leading the movement. He picketed the vice-chancellor and sent a memorandum having seven articles: (*i*) to lodge a criminal case against the members of the Development Council, who're guilty of collapsing the building; (*ii*) higher inquiry into the expenditure under miscellaneous funds; (*iii*) higher enquiry into the expenditure of practical and tour funds; (*iv*) expenditure probe into the library fund; (*v*) enquiry into the Department of Sports; (*vi*) probe into the expenditure of the self-subsidized courses; and (*vii*) probe into all other kinds of expenditure of the students' fees.

On the other hand, Prof. Pandayan, who was the head of the Development Council, was trying secretly to soften him for his tough stand. Prof. Pandayan also met the vice-chancellor and requested him not to accept the demands of Sitaram. He secretly offered Sitaram an *Ambassador* car. He also claimed that all the charges of Sitaram against the council were fictitious and baseless.

Prof. Pandayan submitted a letter to the vice-chancellor and claimed. "... our university is the best in the state. The professors and other staff of the university are very very punctual and dutiful. All the issues in Sitaram's memorandum had already been investigated in the past but not even a single matter of misappropriation came to light. Perhaps the building has collapsed due to the earthquake which came only to its area. None felt it but I'd felt for a moment which collapsed that strong building... the auditors had never objected regarding the misappropriation in the university. All bills and vouchers are available in the office. The *National Assessment And Accreditation Council* has graded it as A+ university. Sitaram wants to destroy the well-established systems of the university. He had begun to disturb us from the beginning of the session. He wants to get us corrupt, but he'll never get success in his motive. Firstly he disturbed Prof Suraj, and then he disturbed Prof Mercy, who were honest men—men of discipline. He remains engaged twenty-four hours against the welfare work of the university. I, therefore, request you to dismiss his demands...."

Fifteen days passed. Sitaram continued his picketing. Therefore, the vice-chancellor accepted his demands and issued an order for a higher enquiry. He appointed a committee having eleven members headed by the Registrar of the university.

The committee began its enquiry and demanded the records of all the issues raised by Sitaram.The bills and vouchers were verified. The committee also investigated the shops and their bills. It took the time of three weeks. The enquiry report was submitted and claimed, "... the committee finds major financial irregularities during the 2000s. Ninety-nine per cent bills are bogus. Except tuition fee, examination fee, mark-sheet and dearness fee, there is misappropriation of ninety-nine per cent amount. Prof Pandayan, Prof Suraj, Prof Mercy... are mainly related to misappropriation. Thirty-seven suppliers are also related to misappropriation, who've issued bogus bills. Mr Bimla is one of them who issued many bogus bills. The librarian has defalcated rupees three lac this year. In this year Prof Mercy has got a *Safari* from Mr Bimla in commission. Most of the bills of the library are bogus. The stickers of higher price are pasted into many books. The books have not been purchased—only their covers have been changed. The same old items are mentioned as newly purchased items on the stock registers of the Department of Sports. The Superintendent of Sports has illegally obtained rupees one lac in cash along with many type of apparel and shoes. In the building 36:01 (sand: cement) for the wall and 18:12:03 (concrete: sand: cement) for the roof was used, hence the building collapsed...."

The enquiry report was submitted to the vice-chancellor. The committee also recommended for another high-level committee to investigate all other issues which were not under its jurisdiction.

Two months passed. No action was taken. So, Sitaram demanded to disclose the report and to take necessary action against the guilty persons. But the vice-chancellor didn't take any action while four months passed of the submission of the report.

When no action was taken Sitaram picketed the vice-chancellor, but he told him that the action will be taken against guilty persons just after the enquiry of the high level committee. But Sitaram was not ready to change his decision. After nine days, the police tried to get him out of the campus forcibly but Sitaram and his supporters flared and began to throw stone to them. Therefore, the police began to beat and some students were wounded. Consequently, they became agitated and burnt many offices of the university. Sitaram and some others were arrested and were sent to the Divisional Jail, Kashi.

CHAPTER

Pillage and the A+ University

The news about all the issues of the university was cast in most of the newspapers. The events in the university raised many questions—one of them was the role of judiciary in democracy. Therefore, the Honourable High Court itself registered a case regarding the issues which were cast in the newspapers and other means of media. The court also ordered the CBI to investigate all the issues. The Joint Director of the agency began his investigation. He demanded all the documents related to the issues and also visited the suppliers and the shops from where bills and vouchers were issued. The expenditure of each kind of fee given by the students and grant of the government given to the university was investigated by the agency. The Joint Director also contacted the students who had read in the university to know about the structure of the university. He also investigated all the vouchers and purchased things for the building along with the things purchased and available in the store of the practical subjects. An enquiry was also held into the store and the office of the Sports Department —its expenditure, auction and useless things. The use of cement, rod, concrete, brick, and sand for the building which was collapsed, was investigated by its experts. He also visited a number of reputed suppliers to know the facts.

After six months of enquiry, he submitted his report to the High Court, "... there is no misappropriation in tuition fee, examination fee, and registration fee.... Except these funds there is major misappropriation in the university. Out of rupees six lac and eighty-one thousand of electricity fee, only rupees twelve thousand has been expended and the rest amount has been misappropriated by Prof. Ram, Prof. Pandayan and Mr Bimla. Out of rupees eight lac of sports fee, only rupees two thousand has been expended for buying sport items and the rest amount has been misappropriated by Prof Ram, Prof. Suraj, Mr Bimla...; and a number of bogus bills and vouchers are enclosed with the records. The development is on the records and there is no development on the spot. The development on the records is only to misappropriate funds. Rupees seven lac has been collected as a library fee. Out of rupees seven lac, only rupees thirty thousand has been expended for purchasing books and the rest amount has been misappropriated by the librarian and others; and the bogus bills and vouchers are tagged with the records. The legal process has not been fulfilled and without tender the books are mentioned purchased only on the records not in the library. Most of the books in the library are useless because they are out of the syllabus and outdated. The stickers of the higher price have been pasted into many books of the library. The old books of the same library have been mentioned as newly purchased books by the librarian and lacs of rupees have been misappropriated. There are many books which are out of the use of the students and have been purchased only to get maximum commission. There is a scarcity of good books and standard books in the library. Rupees fifty thousand of penalty paid by the students for losing and late return of the books has been misappropriated by Mr Sriram, who is a clerk in the library. This amount was never deposited in bank accounts. Rupees two lac of the *study-hall fee* has also been defalcated by the librarian and others. These magazines were supplied to the library by the suppliers which were not sold by them in their shops easily and at last, they were supplied to the library. According to the bills and vouchers available in the library, thirty-five types of magazines and newspapers are purchased but only seven types of magazines and newspapers are available there. Same is the case with the *identity card fee, book bank, audio-visual fee, culture fee, caution money library....* Rupees twelve lac of these funds has been defalcated by the Registrar, the Finance Officer and the members of the Development Council. Rs. twenty lac of *the rowers-rangers fee, NSS fund,* and *tour fee* has been defalcated by Prof Mercy and Prof Soukant, and only Rs two lac is the real expenditure of the above mentioned work. Bogus bills and vouchers are enclosed with the files issued by various suppliers and agencies. Mr Vikrant, Head Clerk, Mr Bhuwan, steno and Mr Bimla are other persons who participated in the defalcation. Some bills and vouchers are hundread times more than the actual price for defalcating money. It is found that Prof Mercy has illegally got an inverter, a pair of shoes, a TV, a refrigerator and a suit for himself in commission—as bribe from Mr Bimla. It is also found that, the self-subsidised courses are held in various departments but only on records, and the list of the teachers and staff of the university for the courses is bogus, and has been made by the heads of the departments only to defalcate money. They've obtained not even a single pice and the payment has been made on the records only.... Rupees three lac has been paid by the university as telephone payments but when the call-lists were verified, the committee came to the conclusion that 99.99 % call numbers were of those people who had no any kind of relation with the university and those calls have been used privately—for private work. Rupees three lac of the miscellaneous fee has been misappropriated by... and bogus bills and... of *TA, DA, tea, sweets* etc are attached to the records. It is a matter of great shame that on the occasions of national festivals like; *Republic Day, Independence Day and*

Gandhi Jayanthi, lacs of rupees have been defalcated previously. On each occasion, rupees five thousand only was expended but bogus bills are attached to the records. In the building, which is collapsed now 36:01 (sand: cement) for the wall and 18:12:03 (concrete: sand: cement) for the roof was used. The brick was also of grade '4'. Therefore, the building collapsed within four days of inauguration and the university authority has illegally got lacs of rupees from the contractor. Hence the committee finds them guilty... and recommends to the Honourable High Court to issue an order to refund rupees eight hundred crore to the university. There were many trees of teak and sal which were cut down by the university authority and were sold illegally but not even a single pice has been deposited in the university accounts. Its small part has been used for their own houses. Therefore, the total amount of rupees twenty-three lac has been defalcated by.... Many acres of land of the university is watery in which water-fruit is grown each year. But not even a single pice is deposited in the university account and total amount of rupees four lac has been misappropriated by the different persons of the university. Some acres of land in the university is used for producing wheat and paddy by some tenants. They deposited money not in the university account but directly they gave it to the university authority. Hence, in last ten years at least rupees thirty lac has been illegally and immorally got by...."

"... is remarkable that regarding some of the above mentioned misappropriation, the departmental investigation had been done eight times, but apart from one committee headed by the Registrar of the university, each committee has investigated partially and has got illegal advantage. During the investigation, about fifty per cent amount of the defalcation amount has been taken from the guilty persons by the members and the head of the investigation committee. So many questions are raised regarding their investigation into the issues. But they continued to save the guilty persons illegally."

"Hence, the committee comes to the conclusion that rupees eight hundred crore in last ten years has been misappropriated by the officers of the university, contractors, suppliers.... So, I recommend the Honourable High Court to penalize them, who are found guilty... after the higher investigation of the committee.... The committee also comes to the conclusion that Sitaram had taken enough wine while he was sitting for picketing before the vice-chancellor, and when the vice-chancellor was trying to soften him, he didn't hear even a single word due to intoxication. Due to this, he along with his supporters became violent and burnt the offices of the university...."

CHAPTER

Assembly Election

After a week Sitaram was sent to the Central Jail from the Divisional Jail, Kashi because a number of persons continued to go to the jail to meet him daily. A number of bail-petitions were moved for the release of Sitaram, but he was not released. Amidst this there was the notification of the by-election for Mubarakpur Assembly Constituency because of the killing of then MLA. Therefore, the Welfare Party authorized him the party candidate for the constituency. Getting him, Sitaram became very very happy. His supporters came to the roads in his support.

In regard of his candidature in the by-election his supporters moved a bail-petition in the Supreme Court requesting to release him to participate in the election campaign but his bail-petition was also rejected there. In spite of the rejection of his bail-petition, he filed his nomination papers to the Returning Officer from the jail. On the day of nomination, there was a huge four-way-cut-out of Sitaram, which was representing Sitaram's presence and a huge crowd was following the *cut-out* on a *gypsy* car. There were also some other four-wheeler and two wheeler vehicles in which his supporters sat. Some of them were moving on feet. A number of loudspeakers were fixed on the vehicles which were producing slogans:

Sitaram is quite clean
None can say, he is mean.

All charges are bogus
Only to withdraw focus.

All Kshatriyas with him
Other candidates are too dim.

Sitaram is not less than fur;
Fate determiner of Mubarakpur.

We've to get him won
And deep root on Maya's bone.

Sitaram is the mightiest
None matches on his set.

Sitaram is the best
Rubbish all the rest.

People chanted these slogans very much loudly. In that very movement it seemed that they were roaring to save the humanity from havoc.

The next day this news was cast in many of the newspapers under the different headings: *Sitaram: A Redeemer, The Best Candidate After Independence, None Can Defeat Him* etc. In most of the newspapers one page was full of his praise which cast his background, his achievements in the university, his future etc.

He remained in the jail but his supporters began his election campaign with full firm and show. They tried to create this faith that Sitaram was the only candidate in the election field who could redeem Mubarakpur. *If he wins the election, Mubarakpur will become the richest and the best area in the state.* They promised the voters, "... as he wins there will be all round development of the constituency and the situation will be changed fully."

Getting the promises made by his supporters, the common people were too happy and hence they began to support him. They also began to participate in election campaign for him.

There was a huge tent just before the election office of Sitaram and his election-in-charge managed vehicles, food and lodging and trucks full of *wine pouches*. The wine expenditure was hundred times more than those of others. The workers kept the pouches in their pockets and worked for him in the field. In the campaign they forgot fully that they had to eat or they'd eaten or not.

After three weeks of campaign, the polling was held. On the day of polling, the workers were in the offices and were fully intoxicated with wine. After three days the counting began and by evening Sitaram was declared victorious. As the result was declared Sitaram's election-in-charge announced, "... only one hundred and seven trucks of pouches in twenty-one days became enough for the victory. If necessary, I was ready to distribute thousands of trucks of wine. They don't know me—what I'm!"

Getting the result of counting Sitaram's heart was swelled with joy and decided to take victory wine—a number of *MacDowell's*. He continued to take it until he couldn't enter full intoxication.

The next morning when he awoke, he went on hunger-strike in the jail for getting a separate room for himself—a separate room was not enough—also for a television, a CD player, a mobile phone etc—freedom to meet each one daily, because he was then a public representative, hence his meeting was in public interest. He was against the action taken by the jail administration against him when his mobile phone was seized.

But the Jail Superintendent was against his demands on legal ground based on the jail manual; and that each prisoner in the jail was equal in regard to facility. Therefore, the Superintendent didn't provide extra-facility for him and he continued his hunger-strike to sit for the picketing.

Within eight days his physical condition became critical. The jail administration tried to soften him, but he didn't change his opinion. So the administration sent him to the civil hospital forcibly. There he was admitted to the emergency ward. After some days he was transferred to the general ward. He was meeting there easily all those, who wanted to meet him. In his ward it seemed that there was a fair where there was a huge crowd. He got thousands of gift packets and his supporters were busy to store them. He was garlanded by the supporters and after this the garlands were kept in the ward. In the meantime, the smell of the flowers was very easily felt and the *hospital smell* was not felt from anywhere. When anyone went to meet him, showing the garlands he said, "They changed my temperament—my mood—my everything."

His supporters wanted to take advantage of his victory. He, therefore, filed a fresh bail-petition in the court for his release. His counsel in the court argued,"... Sitaram's fate has been declared in the election, who's got 99 per cent votes of the votes cast. Now he is a public representative. In the history of *independent India,* except him none has got 99 per cent votes in any direct election. If his bail-petition is not granted, the development works in the area will be affected, which will not be less than the hammers on the spirits of the public. Hence, he should be released in public interest."

His bail-petition was granted and he was released from the jail. After his release, he went to Mubarakpur and arranged a political meeting in the historical *Lohia Maidan.* There he delivered an ideological and philosophical lecture "... *All human things are subject to decay,/And when fate summons monarchs must obey....* Do you get it? Please get it. All worldly things are mortal—either he may be a king or an ordinary man. He has to go from the world definitely. But I've come here for ever not for sometime. But don't mean it unnecessarily. *'Here'* means not on the earth but in Mubarakpur constituency. After independence this is the first time in the history of Mubarakpur that a great socialist leader like Dr. Ram Manohar Lohia is before you and addressing the meeting. Here I promise in this *maidan* that I'll tread the footsteps of Dr. Lohiaji. I'll struggle for the welfare of the people of Mubarakpur—of Uttar Pradesh—of India. I'll struggle in the interest of all mankind. There will be neither partialism nor religionism—neither corruption nor immortality—neither bribery nor misappropriation—neither rape nor murder—neither pillage nor violence....There'll be overflow of *love and brotherhood.* Tiger and goat will drink water together at a time. The tiger will do nothing without the permission of the goat. The tiger will always remain reserved to serve the goat. The goat will also take care of tiger's need—of tiger's problem. This behaviour of the tiger and the goat will be an example—an ideal—a model for the rich and the poor in the world of materialism....; the proletariat for the elite... the elite for the proletariat...."

The next day, he went to the assembly to take vow as a member of the assembly. Having taken vow, he was very soon appointed as minister in the cabinet. Getting it the people—especially of Mubarakpur became very happy. They began to build castle in the air, and said that their leader was not only an MLA but a minister, too—the Development Minister—the minister of the *juicy* department—*creamy* department. They also said, "... whatever he earns, earns for the constituency. His quota of rupees one crore will be used for the welfare of Mubarakpur and other MLAs didn't use accordingly."

Sitaram began to work for his constituency... got a bridge made... two minor canals were dug... the government hospitals in the constituency were repaired... the roads and streets of the city were built and decorated. The quota for one year of one crore ended.

On the other hand, his work of welfare was continued in the whole state. In the general budget, rupees three hundred and fifty three crore was allotted for his ministry but the amount was expended within two months. He, therefore, demanded one another supplementary budget of rupees two thousand crore in the financial year for all round development of the state. Therefore, the government moved one another supplementary budget before the assembly and was passed, too. The amount was expended by him during the period of the next six months for the development work. And there was no amount for the next four months of the financial year. Therefore, he demanded the second supplementary budget. Due to his regular demand, the government moved the second supplementary budget and was passed, too; rupees five hundred crore was sanctioned for his ministry for the next four months but it was expended within the next two months. The government was too much satisfied and pleased with the ministry and released rupees ten thousand crore from the reserved fund itself. But the said amount was soon expended for the work of *welfare* within forty-five days and the ministry had no money for the development works regarding canals, river-banks, roads, etc before the coming rainy season—before the coming monsoon.

In one financial year, he expended rupees three thousand eight hundred and fifty crore which was a record in the history of independent India. A greatest record of the development work by the ministry. His name and ministry was mentioned in the *Limca,* a book of world record. The common people were very happy to know about his performance as a minister. The news about his historical achievement was cast in most of the newspapers usually. The government of the state was very satisfied and decided to award him. The programme was arranged for the motive with full pomp and show. The Chief Minister along with some other ministers visited the programme in which Sitaram was awarded a medal of the *Supreme Minister Award,* along with rupees five lac in cash and a shawl. He was praised too much by the governor and other ministers for the formula applied by him for the development of the state.

The governor addressed the programme and said, "... without any kind of doubt it is quite obvious that Sitaram is the first man after independence, who broke all the records of the development work. The assembly sanctioned the amount four times for the motive. Hence I also present heartiest thanks to the assembly which helped in his development work. In the financial year ten long and wide canals and ten deep and wide ponds were dug. This is not enough? One lac and fifty thousand kms long road was built. Many hospitals and schools were opened and buildings for them were built. Now each village is attached to the roads. Each and every village has been electrified...."

The common people were too much happy. Everywhere and whenever they assembled they began to discuss the achievement of Sitaram in their own ways. They reminded his work in the university. They thought that their leader (Sitaram) was very active as he broke all the past records in the history of the state.

As they were too happy, they considered him as a symbol of their prestige. They felt proud to think that they belonged to such a constituency which was led by a man like Sitaram, who was very popular in the state for the development works and won *Supreme Minister Award.* In the medal he had been remarked H++. 'H' for *historical.* They especially of his constituency began to think and discuss that the former MLA's killing was a boon for the constituency and for the state too, because if he were their MLA, their constituency couldn't get such familiarity as has been done by Sitaram. So they arranged a meeting in Mubarakpur to award Sitaram.

It was the month of *falgun*—two days before *Holi,* a great festival of Hindus. It is considered as the festival of colours. Red and yellow. Pink and green. The wind was very pleasant.

The sun was mild-scorching and sweet-bitter, too. In the very festival of colours, Sitaram was invited by them. He visited there and was awarded the *Jananayake Mubarakpur Samman*, a shawl along with rupees ten lac. He was weighed once equal to roses and once equal to coins. Ninety-nine kgs roses. Ninety-nine kgs coins. He was welcomed by a garland of roses and marigolds. That weighed five kilograms. That was put on his neck. When about a dozen of persons delivered lectures then his turn came at last. Coming to the stage with the garland he began to deliver, "... in this holy place of Mubarakpur in the historical *Lohia Maidan* I take vow that I'll change its colour—but not by colours rather by the development work. I've got plenty of work done in my constituency. Which is not enough. It is a part of my dream. Further I'll make this city as a city of roses as Jaipur is. As you know that previously many people died of starvation. As I know but now none in the state will die of poverty—of cold—of ailment—of disaster. Each house will have air conditioned machine. There will be cold storage in each and every village for farmers. There will have AC facility in each and every school—in each and every college—in each and every hospital. Streets and roads will be pollution free and air conditioned. Are you getting? *Air Conditioned*! I need only your love your co-operation—your support. Nothing else. There will be peace and rest everywhere. No corruption! No! Especially in politics! There will be nothing in the name of corruption in bureaucracy—this is—*eiz my mission*. Please listen to me: *"Now it is beginning of a fight, further there are more fights."*

Most of the people present there were looking not at his face or listening to his lecture but at his garland. They were too much happy and they said, *"Another Ram*! Aha! Sitaram! Sei... taa... ram!" Some of them said, "Aha *Limcaman*! And none was ready there to listen to any word against him.

CHAPTER

Coronation of the Limcaman

The six months passed. Sitaram's work of welfare remained continued. The people of his constituency were satisfied with him and also the people of the whole state. He was popularly known as a *Limcaman*—as a Limcababu among the common people. The Election Commission declared the 14th Assembly Election for all the 445 constituencies of the state. Sitaram was the authorized candidate of the Welfare Party in his constituency. There were seven candidates against him, Sitaram and his supporters began the election publicity with a slogan: *Sitaram winner; others dust-cleaner*. In three weeks of the election publicity it seemed that Sitaram's face and voice was felt even in the sky—in water—everywhere round the clock. Other candidates of the constituency were not popular like Sitaram and were not regarded as him at the doors of the voters. None asked them. But they asked the voters and requested for their support. But as they departed from their doors they began to chant: *Sitaram will win; others will clean.*

A number of articles were written and published in the newspapers and magazines. His interviews were broadcast on radio and television. There was none who said, "Sitaram will lose the election." For the voters the election was only a small formality and they were sure that Sitaram would win the seat.

After the polling the result was announced. Nothing was new in it. Everything was expected. All the candidates against Sitaram lost their security. The victory crown was in his favour. Prof Dudhnath, who was a local candidate against him could get one hundred and seven votes only. It became a subject of the common discussion. They said that in the assembly election there was none except him after independence who had got one hundred and seven votes only. To him, that was a record for getting minimum votes. But in spite of getting the minimum votes he was happy. Not too much. Very much because the people were discussing that his name would be mentioned in the *Limca* in near future.

In the assembly election no political party could get 2/3 majority in the house which was legally necessary for forming the new government. So none could form the new government and the President Rule was imposed. The assembly was suspended. Ramanth was the governor of the state and was supposed to be the supporter of a particular political party. The public said that he was never impartial.

In this way, five months passed and the political leaders tried best to form the government but failed to do so. But fortunately or misfortunately only one hour was rest to extend the President Rule that Sitaram was too eager to form the new government. And just before one hour of the extension of the President Rule he invited the mediamen and declared, "... I'm to get absolute majority to form the government. I'll prove it in the house not on the road. I've formed my own political party named the New Welfare Party. There are seven MLAs in this party out of twenty-one of the Welfare Party. I've been selected the leader of the party. I need the support of only tui... hun... d... red... and... five more members. I declare before the mediamen that I'm now ready to form the government headed by me if other political parties support me. But I'll never get the support of the BPP and other *southists* because it will be against secularism. So they should support me if they want the end of the President Rule and to keep the BPP and other *southists* away from the reign. This will be in the state interest. If they have good idea about their own state they must not lose this golden chance because in lack of *de... mo... cra... tic* government the development of the state is too much low. This year many people died of starvation. As I come to power I'll appoint a judiciary enquiry to find out the real cause of the starvation. The growth rate of the state is lowest in the country only due to the President Rule or in lack of the *de... mo... cra... tic* government. Here I take vow that within the next five years I'll change the fate of the state. I promise it."

Within fifteen minutes seven political parties having two hundred and seventeen members declared their support and sent their support letters to him. He therefore, went to the *Rajbhawan* to meet the governor and to claim to form the government.

As only half an hour was rest for the extension of the president rule, the glance of the people was focussed on the current political development. As the governor knew that Sitaram had formed a new political party having seven members of the assembly, had been elected their leader and had got the support of seven other political parties having two hundred and seventeen MLAs, he left the meeting of the National Security Council headed by the Honourable President and departed from there by a special aeroplane. Getting all the matters of the current political development he legally invited Sitaram for forming the government.

It was 11.55 PM. Sitaram took a vow of the post of the Chief Minister of the state along with all the seven members of the party as cabinet ministers. The president rule ended just after the oath of Sitaram and he took the command of the state in his hand. He was said to prove majority in the House within a month. The time of one month given by the governor was criticized by the leaders of the Opposition parties and they said that the time of one month was given to him only to purchase the *democratic will* of the ML As to prove the majority in the House. They also said that each supporting MLA was getting rupees five crore in cash, a *Safari*, a beautiful and costly mobile set and a golden chance to pass a week with pretty call girls under sixteen in the luxurious hotels wherever or whenever they liked. But Sitaram stand was quite hard and said that the Opposition leaders wanted to blame him and his party; and they were supporting his government according to the inner voice coming from the inner chamber of the heart; and all the charges were baseless and prejudiced. He usually continued to say, "They are afraid of my popularity and they wanted to blur my popularity."

Getting it Madhudatta, who was a reputed BBC correspondent interviewed:

"Are the charges against you regarding the new political stand true or false?"

"Totally false. It is quite baseless—quite imaginary. One can't imagine it. No! Never! You shouldn't forget that I'm Sitaram none else. None else! The media is also not dealing it impartially, while it is the fourth pillar of democracy. They're hungry for power so they're blaming me baselessly. But this is a miracle for them and will never get success in their motive. I'll continue to rule over the state democratically."

"It is true or false that you've paid money to each MLA to get support?"

"Out of imagination. No! Never! The honourable governor has given the time of one month to prove majority in the House, but I'll get the vote of confidence within a week. I don't want to pass one month for this because they'll continue to ill-fame me."

"What is the primary aim of the government?"

"All round development of the state. Equal distribution of the available resources. Justice to each member of each section of the society."

"Do you keep desire to extend your cabinet or your council of ministers after winning the vote of confidence."

"*Yea... as*! Definitely! This is the most relevant question, because the main perspective of the government is all round development; and without proper number of ministers it is quite impossible. So there will be *a jumbo jet* council of ministers which will remain active round the clock for the development of the state."

" It is said that you are offering a *Safari* along with a mobile set having all facilities brought from USA to each MLA who'll support you. Is it true or false?"

"Quite false. No more than this. They're supporting me according to the inner voice coming from the *ei... nna... r* chamber of the heart."

"Among the public it is a matter of common discussion that you're offering *a fairy child full beautiful* under sixteen to each male MLA for seven nights in the luxurious hotels for getting their support. Is it true?"

"Heh! Don't tell me all this. This indecent matter. Heh! Quite imaginary. Is it possible by a man like Sitaram? Never! Only to defame me. None can expect all this by Sitaram. A man like Sitaram."

"May God bless you so that you could change the colour of the state? Thank you."

"Same to you. May God...."

The interview was over. In the same week the meeting of the assembly was called. The government moved a proposal: *this house expresses the vote of confidence.* The government secured the vote of confidence by the voice vote.

And in the same week one hundred and fifty-one MLAs took vow as ministers. Each and every facility of the ministers was provided for them. Then the people in the metropolitan city could know: *red light vehicles, persons in the red light vehicles, VIPs'* and *red light area.* For VIPs' security the streets were often barricaded during the day for the common people. Even they were not free to go out of their houses to perform their daily routine at any time. In the name of high security the people of the city were feeling restless.

Hence, Madhudatta once again visited him for a short interview:

"What is the motive of your jumbo jet council of ministers?"

"Development... development... nothing but only development as I've already declared."

"But according to the constitution only eleven per cent of the assembly members can be appointed as ministers. And you've violated this rule."

"Let it go. I honour the constitution. I honour the law. I've firm faith and blind belief in the constitution. The constitution also knows that I've done all this in interest of the state not in my own interest. The court knows it. When the matter is brought before the court, I'll think... I'll honour...."

Three months passed. He was ruling over the state peacefully. No bustle. No unrest. With peace and rest. No query. No question. No objection. Only dream. But in positive.

But just after three months his dreams turned negative and Deshraj, who was the leader of the Sahara Party withdrew his support saying that *the government failed to maintain law and order in the state.* Therefore, the government is in the minority in the House; and the Opposition leaders began to demand his resignation. But he didn't resign saying that *he would prove his majority in the House not on the road, —not in the streets —not before the media....* He said very boldly, "I've 2/3 majority in the house still. I'll prove it at proper time. Continue to watch over the situation. When the time comes, you'll know it."

Getting the current development in politics the governor asked him to prove majority in the House within fifteen days.

Knowing it Sitaram said, "The governor lacks political will-power. He should give at least two months' time for it because most of the legislators are in the constituencies before the feet of the public and are listening to their woes and miseries. But in spite of all this I'll prove my majority in the house within a week. I'm Sitaram not someone else...."

The session of the House was called on to get the vote of confidence. Before beginning of the session he declared: one who supports me will get... and the post of... in *pub-lic interest* not in my interest. In the House a proposal for the vote of confidence was moved. The debate began. There was a violent uproar. He requested the members to vote for him in the interest of the state according to the voice coming from the inner spirit. The votes were cast and counted. Later announced. The vote of minority. One vote changed his fate. Only one. In spite of all the attempts to get the vote of confidence.

Getting the result he spoke, "... all went. One hundred and twenty-one crore. Was it less? One got but cheated. I'll find out who cheated me...." All this very slowly to an MLA, who had taken contract for his victory.

Before this he had already resigned saying that: *this is the matter of deep distress for the state that in spite of the secret vote based on the inner voice coming from the heart I lost my majority in the house. I, therefore, resign along with the council of ministers...."*

After resignation, the governor asked him to continue the chair till the next order.

Within five days no solution came to light and the cloud of uncertainty remained shaded. But on the sixth day, Deshraj met the governor and claimed to form the new government. He submitted a written letter and said, "... am the leader of the party and two hundred and fifty-four members of the assembly are supporting me unconditionally to form the government. I've got their written support. Here I want to mention that the three MLAs of the *New Welfare Party* have also sent their support letters to me...."

The governor was satisfied with the letters and he invited the members to partake in the parade held in the *rajbhawan*. They participated in it and expressed their support to Deshraj. The governor became satisfied and invited Deshraj to swear and to prove majority in the House within fifteen days. Deshraj took vow of the post along with one hundred and thirty-seven ministers.

After the oath ceremony Madhudatta interviewed him:

"What is the chief priority of the government?"

"Stability of the government."

"No issue of development?"

"It's too. But the second priority."

"There are one hundred and thirty-seven members in the council of ministers. Is it constitutional or not? Do you know it?"

"O Dear Madhudatta! Do you know? This is not the first time. I'm not only one contractor of the constitution. Are you not aware of Sitaram's government. Do you remember the number of the ministers? One hundred and fifty-one. But in my government one hundred and thirty-seven only. Fourteen less than him. It'll be considered later. Now my attention is focused on the stability of the government which is the demand of the state—demand of the time.

"But when you're in Opposition and Shantidoot was the Chief Minister of the state you opposed him saying that *his council of ministers was jumbo jet*."

"Yes! Yes! OK. I remember that even his government had one hundred and twenty-one ministers. But you should also remember that the ministers in his government were too much corrupt, greedy, inactive and... but in mine they've only one motive—motive to serve the people and the state. Service is their only religion. We were supporting Sitaram's government, but he had sold their honesty —the honour of the state —the honour of democracy and the constitution, too. They'd got rupees five crore each along with other things as you know. But in my government none is like his. Now you can imagine the difference between his and mine."

The interview was over.

Deshraj was trying to get the support of the proper number of members. But a new turn in the politics came before getting the vote of confidence in the House. Deshraj couldn't hold even a single meeting of the house but the National Party, which was supporting his government, withdrew its support.

Ekbal, who was the President of the party withdrew the support and said,"... Deshraj has violated the oral agreement. According to the agreement each member of my party had to become the minister in his cabinet and I'd to be the Deputy Chief Minister of the state. But Deshraj has violated the agreement and only forty-three out of forty-seven members of the party could have become ministers in his cabinet. I, therefore, withdraw my support."

In spite of the withdrawal of his support, Deshraj didn't resign the post but began to deliver political hymns and said, "... the government is not in minority, still. Who says? I say that I'm in majority and I'll prove it in the assembly. I've 2/3 majority in the assembly. You should know it that some members of each party even some independent members are in my support—in my favour and while voting they'll vote according to their own will not according to their party whips. The next day my government is going to prove majority in the assembly."

It was Monday. The day for getting the vote of confidence. The government moved the proposal of one line to prove majority in the House. The debate began. It continued for six hours. During the period Deshraj was silent and trying to judge the mood of the MLAs. The ministers were arguing on behalf of him. When he became aware of the intention of the members, he resigned before casting the votes.

With his resignation, the market of the politics was opened. There was a week. The week of marketing. Sitaram was the best customer of the industry as the people said.

As the week had passed that Sitaram went to the *Rajbhawan* and claimed to form the government.

He claimed, "Once again I claim to form the government after getting the support of two hundred and forty-five members. I've got their support in written ways which are attached to the letter. I've firm faith that the new government will be able to fulfil the five year term of the assembly.

Having considered all the issues he once again invited Sitaram to form the government. The next day Sitaram reached the *Rajbhawan* and took vow as a Chief Minister. The three members who had once left the *New Welfare Party* and were supporting Deshraj's government also swore the new government as ministers.

CHAPTER

Right to Information

Sitaram once again became the Chief Minister of the state but the cloud of uncertainly began to float. Only thirteen days had passed that the Opposition leaders began to demand the disclosure of the report of the committee regarding the murder of Maya, former MLA of Mubarakpur constituency but he was not ready to do so. With this demand he lost peace and rest of his life. He came to the ground along with his dreams. His hopes turned into pieces. He turned too pale—became lean and thin. He spoke very cautiously and slowly. He visited his office daily but no new policy—no new idea—only in search of the solution of the problem. Lovely, his cousin's wife was also very anxious and she usually asked him, what's happened?"

Saying it she chanted the first stanza of John Keats' *La Belle Dame Sans Merci:*

O what can ail thee, knight-at-arms,
Alone and palely loitering?
The sedge has wither'd from the lake,
And no birds sing.

The demand for its disclosure remained continued but the government was not ready to disclose it in the name of the security matter. The government said, "... the *police investigation* is continued still and if it is disclosed the investigation work may be affected." It was quite clear that the government was not ready to do so; and both the government and the opposition party were advocating their own stand. The government said that it had no intention to save anyone and as the final investigation report of the police comes it would be kept on the table of the house for common discussion.

The Opposition leaders were not ready to change their stand. The assembly was in session. They, therefore, made a noise in it for the fulfilment of the purpose. They set-backed the session to table the report. It was not enough for them but also quarrelled with the members of the ruling party; and at least one hundred and eighty-three members were badly wounded. Some new furniture and seventy-two microphones were also broken. The speaker of the assembly was also badly wounded.

In spite of all this, there was no enquiry—no case—only oral charges against one another. In this respect they said that it was the matter of the assembly and couldn't be discussed out of it. In the media, the news was cast too much and in the editorials the editors were claiming that the members were ill-faming holy Democracy and the House both. The common people were not too much behind them and they were also criticizing for such misdeeds. They said that they were burden on democracy—the same democracy which had awarded equal chance to the citizens of India. They also said that they're dealing politics as game only for the fulfilment of their lust.

This news had not gone out of the media that one another event occurred. Sitaram was trying to commit suicide having hanged himself from the hook of the ceiling. But his life was saved by Lovely. The news tore all the news among the media and it became the matter of the common discussion. Lovely got him admitted to a private hospital secretly but the secret was broken out by the mediamen and they interviewed her.

Before them she replied angrily, "What can I say? I can say nothing. All of you know what is the matter? They want to ill-fame him... to blur his popularity. They want to disturb the government. In the assembly he has been wounded. The private part of his body has been wounded badly which I know only. Not someone else. They've no shame and even they don't care for the private part of the body during the tussle. And they're MLAs—*faemalays.* He is an honest man. Quite honest. Even a single pice can't be got by him illegally. He is serving the state—the people of the state. He gets nothing for his service. He gets rupee one only for his service as token pay. Only due to him there is all round development of the state otherwise....And you—all of you don't care about him—publish news against him. Have you no shame? You've come here to see him. Go out of the ward. He'll speak nothing to you. Have you tears; or crocodile tears for him? Say to me. Why not? I say, go out. I say. I...."

All this was cast in most of the daily newspapers. Getting it some people especially of his constituency believed that their leader who was a quite honest man by birth, had become prey of the bad intention of the Opposition leaders. On the other hand, some people were against him and began to believe that Sitaram had committed something wrong which was unknown by the common people. But it was quite obvious that about ninety-nine per cent people of his constituency and ninety per cent people out of the constituency were his supporters then, too; and were not ready to read the newspapers describing anything against him.

In the very week a new turn came to the history of Indian democracy that the Central Government passed a bill: *Right to Information* and it became law. Getting it Deshraj, who was a member of the assembly applied to get the report of the committee under the law. But his application was rejected saying that *this is the matter of security*....

So Deshraj lodged an appeal before the *State Information Commission* against the order. His case was heard there and lasted for only a week. After the hearing the judgement was delivered, "This is the matter of an incomplete investiga-tion. The investigation by the police is continued still. If the report of the committee is disclosed the investigation will be affected. This is also a matter of the assembly so it can be discussed only in it. It'll be the violation of the special right of the assembly. So it doesn't come under the law of *Right to Information*. Hence the appeal is dismissed."

Knowing it political leaders began to oppose the decision of the *State Information Commission*. They claimed that the officer was prejudiced and due to the prejudice he had dismissed the appeal of Deshraj. They considered the decision unconstitutional which deprived Deshraj of his fundamental rights. But Deshraj was not ready to accept his defeat and filed a case in the High Court against the decision.

In the court his case was admitted. After three months, the hearing of the case began.

Awanish, who was the counsel for Deshraj in the court said, "... now the *Right to Information* is a fundamental right. None can deprive him of it. According to the law anyone can get any kind of information except the information related to the national security. His demand is legal and if it is disclosed it will not be illegal but bad intentions and guilt of the person(s) will come to light. The victim will get justice which is very necessary for democracy. It, therefore, must be disclosed."

Manish was the counsel for the..., who was against his demand, tried too, to prove that the demand of Deshraj was illegal and the report can't be disclosed till the report of the final investigation.

He claimed in the court, "This is the matter of security. Not an ordinary matter. This report can be considered as an interim report because the police investigation is continued still. There are some other factors, too. Therefore, none can be permitted to get its copy...."

Finally, the judgement came which was expected because the Central Government was beating its own drum; of the *Right to Information*. The judgment was delivered in favour of Deshraj.

"... the bench considered all the aspects of the case seriously and comes to the conclusion that... this is not the matter of security and the *State Information Commission* has delivered its decision against Deshraj because of the illegal pressure of the state government. There is no problem to disclose the report of the committee. Hence the court orders the *State Information Commission* to issue a copy of the report to Deshraj within a week."

After the favourable decision Deshraj was silent and waiting for the compliance of the order of the court but when a week passed and he didn't get the copy of the report, he went to the office of the commission to find out the causes of the delay, and knew that the Secretary of the *State Information Commission* had been transferred by the government and there was no officer on his behalf; and the post was vacant.

CHAPTER

Religion for Scandal

The former government of the state had appointed a commission to estimate the religions like; Hinduism, Islam, Christianity, Sikh, Jainism and Buddhism... and also to judge their activities in the religious centres.

The commission began to work. It visited several religious centres related to the different religions and also the education centres which were run by the religious boards or institutions. It contacted their authorities and followers, too. At least one village in one district was necessary to visit and to judge the situation. The commission had also to contact each authority related to religion from bottom to top.

About a year passed. It prepared the report with the help of the other four members belonging to the different religions. The report was submitted to the government.

"There is too much hypocrisy in Hinduism. Practically more—ideologically less. There is corruption in the temples also too much. Mostly in the well-known temples. The priest themselves exploit their own clients—the devotees. They also misbehave. They are robbed, too. They go to the temples to get the boon—to get the blessing but they are looted and cheated by the priests—especially by the hypocritic priests.

The priests use them—deal them as milch-cows. Some priests also have extra-marital relations. They seem physically priests but their acts are like butchers. They pass their lives luxuriously. Getting the chance some corrupt priests rape and kidnap the women. They also sexually abuse them. They mix intoxicating things with the *prasad* (holy food) for the devotees and when they become intoxicated they rape the women and the girls. Their domestic life is *clotted* not only blotted. But it happens to some well-known or famous temples not to the ordinary temples. The seers are not petty corrupt. They commit everything they can in broad daylight and in the thick darkness of night, too. No shame. No hesitation. No fear. Only chance. They murder and get the virtuous priests and the devotees murdered, who obstruct their way of corruption—their evils. There are a number of cases in the courts being instituted against them. Some monasteries have become corruption centres instead of religious centres. They don't consist even a single virtue of a seer...."

"... Islam is not too much behind... and some people said that there is intolerance—too intolerance and extreism in it. But the Holy Quran doesn't allow it—Islam doesn't allow it. The mosque is definitely a holy place.... Nowadays some education centres have become study centres of extremism and violence. Undoubtedly the religious persons are good men but some of them participate in violence and blood-shed. They're violent and extremist. Their private life is not pure and they live luxuriously. Some of them are related to the terrorism. But definitely most of them are virtuous.... They are humanist. Some centres and some extremist groups are also nurtured by Pakistan's intelligence agency ISI, which creates an atmosphere of fear and terror not only in the state but all over the country...."

"Except some cases, there is no corruption in churches. They're holy places ideologically and practically, too. Priests coach devotees the lesson of humanism, love and brotherhood. Love is the essence of religion—of Christianity. The priests are virtuous...."

" The Christian community runs a number of educational institutions like—schools and colleges not only in advanced areas but also in backward areas—especially in the tribal areas where socially and educationally backward people live. They are served by the Christian community and later they convert themselves from Hinduism to Christianity. For the fulfilment of the purpose, the community uses the weapon of love and service. Consequently lacs of Hindus change their religion and become Christian every year, but most of them are related to the schedule castes and schedule tribes—not to the upper castes or middle castes."

"The Sikh Temples are holy and there is less corruption there. This religion teaches us the lesson of sacrifice and human service. *Granthis* in the Sikh temples teach its extracts and are virtuous. There is neither extremism nor intolerance in it. They don't participate in unsocial, illegal, and unreligious activities. They work in religious, human, social and national interest. There is no danger of the nation because of the Sikh religion."

"Buddhist Temples are also holy places and there is neither corruption nor cheating. No debauchery, too. They win the hearts of the devotees; and they are minority in the state. One thing is very important here. There are many Buddhists who've been converted from Hinduism (and mainly who belonged to the schedule castes), take advantage of the government policy illegally while there is no caste system in Buddhism. Same is the case with Christianity and Islam. They cheat themselves, society, law, constitution, state and finally God. Hence they must be deprived of the government reservation policy as well as other policies providing advantage. There must be a special law for their deprivation so that none could cheat the constitution.... I recommend for the hard and fast rule regarding this as soon as possible. If the government doesn't take immediate step regarding this it will become a matter against the national interest, because in the name of freedom of religion some unsocial elements enter the country and extend their activities in the name of the religious programmes. In another way the neighbouring countries are preparing an ideological field for future."

"... Jain Temples are mostly in cities. Its followers are spread all over the country. They remain busy with their own work. They don't take interest in destructive work. The priests are also virtuous. They are in minority...."

"... all other religions and their followers are in minority. There is no need to take any kind of action against them. The Civil Code of Conduct should be enforced all over the country. Most of the people don't know about the supreme religion of all mankind. Non-violence, love, brotherhood, pity, sympathy, tolerance... nothing for them."

Getting the report, the government itself tabled it in the assembly for debate. The news was cast by the media. People became aware of the report. It was warmly welcomed. It became the most important issue among the public—in the assembly. The means of media was also giving it the chiefest priority. The news regarding it, Sitaram was reading smilingly. There was a rosy smile on his cheeks.

Some people were getting it as the flash to remove the attention from the main issue. They said that the government had knowingly tabled the report in the assembly so that the attention of the media, of the political leaders and of the common people could be removed from the main issue—the issue regarding the disclosure of the report of the murder of then MLA of Mubarakpur.

Only a week had passed that it happened a violence in which eighty-eight people of the upper castes belonging to the *Veer Sena,* which was an illegal and underground social party supposed to be of the upper castes were killed in a remote village of the state by the *RCC,* which was one another illegal underground social party which was supposed to be the party of the lower castes, along with some poor people of the upper castes. Hence the situation became tense all over the state. About three lac troops were deployed all over the state to maintain law and order. The governor also visited the spot to judge the situation. Getting back to the *rajbhawan* he sent his report to the President of India and recommended to dismiss the state government.

The President was out of the country to participate in an International meeting for the abolition of poverty. Therefore, the report was faxed to him from his office and from there he dismissed the government and imposed the President Rule saying, "... *the state government has failed to maintain law and order in the state and to defend the constitution.This is the failure of the government. Three racial riots have been taken place this year. Therefore, the state government is dismissed....*"

Only one week had passed that the government appointed Akhilesh as a Secretary of the *State Information Commission* against the post which was vacant due to the transfer of the ex-secretary of the commission.

The second day of his appointment he issued a copy of the report regarding the murder of then MLA of Mubarakpur to Deshraj.

Deshraj distributed it to the mediamen. The main points were published in some of the newspapers:

> "It is a matter of conspiracy. It is quite obvious. None can ignore it. Sitaram is involved in it and has got him murdered by.... He had hired the murderers and had paid rupees ten lac. Dodi...who was a notorious criminal had got its contract but they were beyond the reach of the police and were living under Sitaram's protection. The names of the accused in the police case are the names of those persons, who were quite unaware of the event and knew nothing about the murder of the MLA. They are quite innocent obviously. Now, they are in the Central Jail, Mubarakpur."

This report was published in the newspapers and was broadcast on radio and some TV news channels. Knowing it the people turned agitated and the whole state was flung into the fire. A number of protest marches were held. Different political parties, social activists and the public picketed the government institutions. Eighty passenger trains were burnt. One hundred and eighty-seven railway stations and bus depots were burnt. Three hundred and seventy offices and about six hundred government and non-government buses were also burnt. Three hundred and two persons were killed. The violence continued over a month.

People demanded Sitaram's arrest. But Sitaram condemned all this and said very boldly, "All this is a conspiracy of the leaders of the Opposition parties who want to put black spot on my character. The fact is that I know nothing about all this. Who killed him God knows, not I. In my life I've not got even a rat murdered. They are defaming me for the political mileage—for the political advantage. People are misguided by the Opposition leaders and others, too. Soon they will be noticed the facts and will come in my support. They're with me still, but they have been misguided...."

But in such a situation none was ready to listen to Sitaram and he was arrested. He was sent to the Central Jail. But soon after his arrest, he expressed pain in his abdomen, the court, therefore sent him to the government hospital. There he began to enjoy everything possible—a well-decorated bedroom, a sofa set, a colour TV with the VCD, a cellular phone etc, and everything in an air conditioned room.

It was also said that he went home at night and came back at dawn. A number of persons meet him daily. From there he ran the office of his party as the people said and he directed the supporters.

The Opposition leaders said that he was not ill and pretended to be ill only to pass time in the hospital in the name of treatment—the medical report of his ailment was also false.

Getting it, the government appointed a high level medical team to investigate his ailment. So, they investigated his ailment and noticed that he was not ill and pretended to be ill. As the report was submitted, the government took quick action and ordered to send him to prison. The next day he was sent there.

On the other hand, he was trying to be released from the jail and he filed bail-petitions in the courts but the petitions were dismissed in the Lower Court and the High Court.

But in spite of all this he didn't leave his attempt and filed a bail-petition in the Supreme Court. After several dates of hearing, the court granted his bail and he came out of the jail.

Coming out of the jail he addressed the media, "I've firm faith—*faarm* faith in law and the constitution. I'm not guilty. All the charges against me are baseless and prejudiced only to blur my popularity. But I'm a leader of the Earth. None can harm me—defeat me. Very soon they'll stand aside and I'll get a clean chit by the court as I'm quite innocent. I'm guiltless. I say once again that I've not got even a rat murdered—or have murdered in my whole life...."

CHAPTER

Election for Only Stability

The BPP, which was a national level political party withdrew its support from the Central Government. So the then central government lost its majority in the House just after sixty-three days of the formation of the government. In this regard, the President of India told the government to prove the majority in the House within fifteen days.

With respect to the order, the government arranged an emergency session of the *Lok Sabha* to get the vote of confidence. The proposal of one line was tabled in the House. The debate began and continued for twelve hours. Later the vote was cast and counted, too. In the confidential voting there were two hundred and fifty votes for and two hundred seventy against the motion. As it was declared, the Prime Minister along with his cabinet resigned. The President accepted his resignation and dismissed the *Lok Sabha*. The mid-term poll was declared. The political leaders began to cultivate not their bodies but also their minds and hearts to get political friends; leaders and parties; and then they forgot everything in the name of political alliance—except one thing—that was the political mileage. Many inactive leaders came to the stage with the Gandhi-cap, *dhoti and kurta*. All began to deliver political ideology and to chant political slogans. The sale of the portraits of the great patriot leaders like—M Gandhi, Subhas Chandra Bose, J L Nehru, G K Gokhale, B G Tilak, B R Ambedkar, Jatin Das, Bhagat Singh, C Azad and others was on the increase. They began to discuss the matters of national security and integrity, rape, murder, illiteracy, poverty, starvation, social justice, social security... in their own ways.

They declared their own manifestos—roses like attractive manifestos. All were united in three fronts; the National Front, the United Front and the Third Front; and in the Third Front there were thirty-nine political parties—national and regional.

The National Front was headed by the INC (P) which declared, "... the party or the front will provide the stable government for the term of five years—full five years, education to everybody, employment for everybody, 17 per cent development rate, 10 per cent reservation for the minority, water for irrigation in each field, at least 60 litres of pure water for everybody, lavatory in each village, social security, social harmony, special protection scheme for SC and ST, free education to each child below 14 years of age, free education to women, privatization of companies, economic reformation and liberalization, peace dialogue with Pakistan...."

Reading the manifesto people were happy—especially the minority community as there was the provision of 10 per cent reservation for them in the manifesto.

The people said, "... The INC (P) had played important role for the freedom of the country and had provided the stable governments for about forty years after independence; and except it none could provide the stable government. It is the party of Gandhi, Nehru and other great patriotic leaders. Other factions of the multi-political parties can't provide the stable government. None has right to rule over the country except INC (P) as it had served our country. Its members were great patriot and still...."

The BPP which was leading the United Front, was behind the National Front but not too much behind and declared its own manifesto, "... foundation of the *Shriram Temple* in Ayodhya, abolition of the Article 370 from the constitution, everybody will be at least a millionaire, salvation of the *Shrikrishna Temple* in Mathura, salvation of the *Baba Vishvanath Temple* in Kashi, 10 per cent reservation for economically Backward Class among the Upper Castes, implementation of the civil code of conduct, new constitution, establishment of the *Ram-Rajya,* declaration of the Hindu state, end of the cow slaughter, education to everybody, new education policy, at least 100 litres of pure water for everybody who live in cities, national integrity, security to everybody, provision to prohibit the citizen of the foreign origin on the higher constitutional posts, attainment of the Pakistan occupied Kashmir, hard and fast rule to end terrorism from India, peace process with Pakistan, social justice, social security, water for irrigation, social harmony...."

It was published in most of the daily newspapers and its copies were also distributed among the public. Mostly Hindus were happy to the manifesto but especially the people of the Upper Castes. Their reaction was positive.

"... only BPP can make India a Hindu state, the *Shriram Temple* in Ayodhya will be built. The civil code of conduct will be implemented—people of any community will reside alike, live and seem alike. The INC (P) has failed to provide minimum requirements for the common people although ruled over the country for about forty years. There will be well-maintained roads and even the remote villages will be attached to them. There will be social harmony—*Ram-Rajya.* Neither violence nor bloodshed. Neither exploitation nor suppression. Neither poverty nor starvation. Everybody will be at least a millionaire. No conversion as lacs of Hindus change their religion each year. This is our own party—a party of the Hindus—a party of the *matribhumi....*"

The Third Front was more serious to form the new government in national interest as was claimed. Its manifesto was also bulky and alluring.

"... end of partialism, the national government having regional parties, participation of the common people in the government, common minimum programme, new pay commission, new economic policy for the poor, new education policy, social security, social harmony, social justice, caste system for welfare work, welfare policy for Schedule Castes, Schedule Tribes and OBCs, pure water for everybody, electricity in each part of the country, extension of the railway tracks, extension of the roads, national security, end of terrorism, beginning of peace process with Pakistan, good relation with world powers, appointment of *Lokpal*, education as a fundamental right, right to information, free education to women, end of the company-raj, necessary requirements to declare property of the members of the parliament and the assembly, and also of the officers of the public sector, special provision for the weaker sections of the society, 18 per cent interest-rate on GPF, welfare work for physically challenged persons...."

The manifesto left attractive sign on the voters. Its supporters were mostly the people of the Lower Class. They became very happy. Their reaction was more positive than that of others.

"... this front is the party of the poor... until now the country is ruled by only 4 per cent people of the country. There is corruption everywhere. The front represents all the parts of our country—from north to south—from east to west—from Kashmir to Kanyakumari—from Bengal to Amritsar. Hence, the front is better than others. This is the demand of the time...," they said.

The leftists who were the part of the front issued their own manifestos separately, "... end of capitalism, end of imperialism, equal distribution of wealth and reign, end of evils—bribery, corruption, rape, murder, poverty, exploitation, suppression etc., 150 litres of pure water to everybody, free water in each field, proper wage, guarantee of employment, free education to each citizen, system of *Panchayatiraj*, decentralization of reign, national security and integrity, humanism, freedom of religion, patriotism, economic reformation, communalism, free electricity in rural areas, end of the company-*raj,* No place for the World Bank and foreign companies in India, distance from USA...."

There was not so much impact of the manifesto as they said that the manifesto was traditional which had been issued from time to time after independence, but they believed that it was very much important for the Equality Based Society and for all round development and peace of the country.

Its supporters were very few in number but reacted very boldly, "... in spite of no influence of the leftists in the country except West Bengal, Kerala... the manifesto is relevant. Only the leftists can work for the development, social harmony, equal distribution of wealth, social unity, social justice, social security and for the abolition of sectarianism, partialism, exploitation, suppression, rape, murder, bribery etc. They are the parties of labourers and farmers, indeed. Others fail to award justice...."

The New Welfare Party headed by Sitaram was fighting for thirty-seven constituencies under the banner of the Third Front. Sitaram also participated in the election campaign with the leaders of the front and addressed many meetings.

He usually delivered, "... I'm in the Third Front not to gain but only to change the fate of the country. As you know that the charges against me were false and prejudiced only to defame me. I know that you're aware of the facts. If you help me in this election, I'll change the fate of the country. You must know that I'm Sitaram...."

Knowing it, the public once again began to believe, "All the charges against him were baseless. Indeed he is an honest politician. His face is just like Mahatma Gandhi and his long hands, too. The long hands are the symbol of an incarnate man as we know that the hands of the most of the Hindu incarnations were long. He'll really change the country. There will be plenty of love and brotherhood... everywhere...."

But the people of his native state were not ready to believe him like the people of the other states. They're suspicious and they didn't support him as in the past. He had to face strong protest in his constituencies. So he contested for four seats—Jabalpur, Mithapur, Newganj and Pratappur. In spite of his great endeavour he could win only one seat—the seat of Mithapur.

The election process continued for three months, which was a record in the history of independent India. Three hundred and sixty-one people were killed in the election over the country. One thousand and seven persons were injured. One thousand and forty-seven cases were registered because of the violation of the code of conduct. About two thousand people were arrested.

After this long election-process, votes were counted and the results were declared. No party or front could get the proper number of seats to form the government. That was hung parliament.

The result was that none could form the new government. The give and take policy began. The market was very hot as the people said. The rate was also too high—in crores.

The political parties began to make new alliances. They tried to get the new participants for the new government.

For the fulfilment of the purpose they usually said, "... is not wrong. This is the demand of the present time and some members are changing their front to fulfil the *deshdharma*—to fulfil the *sambidhandharma* based on the similar ideology and the voice coming from the inner chamber of the heart. It's in the national interest...."

In spite of all the attempts made by them they failed to form the government. Hence, the President arranged a all-party meeting to discuss the current political situation. After the discussion he suggested them to form the national government in national interest so that the country could be exempted from one another parliamentary election—the by-election. Many leaders agreed with him and were ready to do in regard of the President's suggestion. But some leaders didn't agree with him and demanded more time of fifteen days. So he granted their request.

The marketing process began once again with great zeal and patience. There was hike of the price. All the old and the new fronts or parties participated in the process and they changed their own fates. The *give and take* policy was adopted.

The INC (P) argued, "... this is the only party in the parliament having maximum seats and has got the mandate to form the new government. Therefore, the other parties of the same ideology should support it."

"The BPP was also eager to form the government. It argued, "... INC (P) has ruled over the country for about forty years, but failed to give social justice to the common people. There is corruption everywhere in the country. Thirty-five per cent of people who belong to the *Below Poverty Line* live miserably. There is no water for irrigation. There is the stigma of illiteracy in rural areas and the INC (P) has failed to provide education for all citizens. The representation of SC, ST and OBC in the government services is very poor. The INC (P) is not a political party, indeed, but a family party of Gandhi-Nehru family which is a black spot on any democratic country like India. There are many charges against its leaders. The party doesn't care about the Hindus and they live as refugees in their own country. The party has done nothing for SC, ST, and OBC.... So it has no moral right to form the government. It is mere imagination that the Third Front can provide stable government to the country, which is the call of the time. So only BPP has moral right and ability to form the government and the President should certainly invite it to do so...."

But there was a very hard and fast reaction in INC(P) for it, "The BPP wants to divide the country into pieces in the name of religion. It wants to destruct the country as the slogan of the party is: *Hinduraj-Hindudesh*. Indeed the BPP doesn't want to establish *Hinduraj* and *Hindudesh* but only the *Brahminraj*, a *rajya* which will be ruled only by the Brahmins, the upper most caste and some others who belong to the rich community among the Hindus. It has anxiety only about them who are Hindus in its view practically but never for SC, ST, OBC and minorities. They must know that the only INC(P) has provided social justice, social security and social harmony —and has also provided *food, clothes* and *houses* for each and every citizen of India. There are lacs of educational institutions spread all over the country for higher education which produces scientists, doctors, teachers, officers and civilized citizens. The government of only my party have defeated Pakistan three times—and have founded factories, companies, hospitals and other necessary organizations too. Hence, only this party has moral right and ability, too, to form the government."

The Third Front tried to get the support and to form the government in the name of representation of most of the regional parties and the national parties. It was also too eager and requested the INC (P) along with some other parties to support it.

"... here... now... INC(P) is committing a blunder and should consider the matter seriously otherwise the blunder will destroy the future of the party and the BPP will occupy the reign of the country. The Third Front is also committed to provide the stable government which is in national interest. The voters have given the verdict to us not to the INC (P) or the BPP. This is the first time in the history of independent India that the verdict is in the favour of the front and the leftists.... So they must support the front, who believe in its ideology."

In this way, thirteen days passed out of the fifteen days. Each and every party or alliance tried its luck to form the new government but failed, and the Third Front won the race.

The INC (P) couldn't become ready to support it but the BPP did so conditionally and outwardly. It was the day— the fifteenth day when Akashraj, who was the leader of the front took vow in the historical Ashok Hall and formed the new government. Thirty-nine political parties having two hundred and seventy-five members supported it. There were one hundred and fifty-one members in the council of ministers; and the people said that it was the demand of the contemporary politics.

Three weeks passed. The Prime Minister couldn't allot the portfolios to the ministers as most of them were interested to get *malaidar, rasdar* and *mansal* portfolios. None was ready to accept the portfolios of Textile Minister, Disaster Management Minister, and Desert Minister... but everybody tried to get the portfolios of Finance Minister, External-Affairs Minister, Home Minister, Defence Minister, Railway Minister....So the Prime Minister himself held all the ministries for a long time and said that there was too much delay for the allotment of the portfolios as he was in search of able among ablest for each ministry in national interest.

But INC (P) opposed the government saying that "... The Third Front along with the BPP has cheated the verdict and in the next election my party will get the full majority."

Anyhow after eighteen days the portfolios were allotted; and on the twentieth day the government could get the vote of confidence in the House.

Sitaram was given the Ministry of Disaster Management but he didn't accept it. He filled with rage and said, "... I needn't the Ministry of Disaster Management as there is no need of such a man like me for it. Only the Home Ministry suits me; and I am committed to do so at any cost. I want to get only this portfolio otherwise I'll resign from the cabinet. My inner voice suggests me only to get this ministry so that I can use my experiences and to the best of my capacity for the welfare of the people—for the welfare of the country. I know none can forbid me to do so; and if it is done the government will not prolong even for a single day.... I say. The Prime Minister should know this. The welfare of the poor is quite impossible without me. Within twenty-four hours it should be changed... otherwise...."

But the Prime Minister was not ready to change his portfolio as a dozen of ministers demanded the change and didn't hold the ministries. They also threatened to do the same.

On the other hand, the Opposition leaders were criticizing the government on different levels. They also said that Sitaram took interest in the Home Ministry because of some certain reasons which would be noticed in course of time.

Twenty-four hours passed. His ministry was not changed. So he went before the media to declare his stand.

He said, "Now twenty-four minutes more to reconsider the issue—*twen... ty -four* minutes only, not twenty-five minutes or even a second. I'm Sitaram. I say... I say...."

Getting the hard decision of Sitaram the Prime Minister discussed the issue with the other ministers and sent an SMS, "... will be very very pleased to know that you're as a Home Minister now—not as a Disaster Management Minister in the cabinet...."

10

CHAPTER

Home Ministry and Red Light Men

Sitaram occupied the post of the Home Minister and continued to sit in the ministry regularly. Because of the pressure of Deshraj and other members of the House he ordered his secretary to prepare a plan with the Law Ministry for the quick disposal of the criminal cases all over the country to abolish corruption. He appointed a *five-member* committee to do so. The committee began to work from the second day of the appointment.

He also requested the Prime Minister to provide a special car for him—a special car having special signs so that he would be recognized easily by the public as he was going to change the fate of the country.

He suggested, "... lights all around the car... sixes... in one side... but one more in the front side—bigger size in the middle of the sixes... all this for the Home Minister in Home... not out of home...."

As there was no rule for this type of facility, the government firstly issued a notification just after an emergency meeting of the cabinet, "... in regard of the request of the Home Minister the cabinet discusses the issue seriously, the government provides a special car having two dozen lights along with a bigger light in the front side in national interest as he is committed to abolish corruption from the country—the most serious problem...."

The special car was given to him. He began his work of welfare. The people said that he had begun his work with full courage and zeal. He was popularly known as a *Red Lightman* among the public and visited several states and addressed thousands of meetings of the different departments.

In the meeting he continued to say usually:

"I'm committed to abolish hundred per cent of corruption from the country. I accept this challenge heartily. Indeed this is the most serious problem of the country. The leaders are corrupt... officers are corrupt... all are corrupt... but I'm not... not I'm... it is the greatest evil. Without its abolition, the welfare of the country is quite impossible. If I fail to abolish it, none can do it. But don't worry, within five years there will be no sign of corruption in the country. Nothing will be in the name of crime. There will be virtues... only virtue. In near future the fallen needle will reach its master automatically. None will harm anyone. There will be love and brotherhood everywhere...."

When one year of his untiring effort to abolish corruption passed, the people were very happy. The media cast usually, "... Sitaram : the first man in the history of the world who addressed four thousand seven hundred and forty-three meetings for the abolition of corruption—to build new India—India of the 25th century—25th century of the Superman...."

Usually this type of news was published by the newspapers and broadcast on AIR & TV channels.

His name had been recorded in the Guinness Book along with a passport size photograph, and in the bottom it was written: *Sitaram: The Enemy of Corruption.*"

In those days there was one another news regarding him which was published on the front page in most in of the daily newspapers, which was the subject of public discussion everywhere—in the streets—in the trains—in the offices:

"A *balbrahmchari*, who didn't marry whole life, who sacrificed his life for the country—for the *matribhumi*—for the poor—for the helpless people—for the redemption of Mother India from corruption. While he is out of station, he stays in cheap hotels—takes bath by *lota* and *balti* made of brass, not by jug and tub. He never stays in luxurious hotels like others and never enjoys call-girls. Whenever he addresses international organizations, he speaks and delivers lectures in Hindi—in Mother Tongue... never in English or in other foreign languages. Indeed, he is a redeemer...."

The market of the newspapers was in highest profit as the people read them to get any news regarding Sitaram. Its market increased. The new customers joined the market—also of the rural areas. The reading of the newspapers became a status symbol.

The mediamen were happy to get such a golden chance for the printed media in the electronic age as the increase of the sale—increase of the new readers. Therefore, they took interest to publish any news regarding him. Only due to their efforts the situation was that getting the newspapers the readers read firstly anything about Sitaram. While playing radio they listened to the news only about him and then switched off.

Later the situation was that they published and cast all the news from the birth of his seventh grand-father to the Home Ministry and they had no news to cast, but the people were as eager as in the past. So they began to cast the news about his seat of taking food.

The Mirror of Leaders, which was a national level newspaper cast the news on the front page under heading; *Hindu rastra-Hindu culture:*

"He wears a white loin-cloth and a banian. All are handmade of the Gandhi Ashram, an organization which produces handmade-cotton cloth. He is a true Indian and buys Indian clothes. He follows *'Be Indian; Buy Indian.'* There are three auspicious lines of sandal-wood paste on his forehead. He sits on a mat made of *kush* not on the luxurious cushion. The mat was made by the weavers of his own village. He is the supporter of the small-scale industry. He eats only two *chapattis* in a dish not in a plate and drinks 200 ml water from a bowl not from a glass. While eating he doesn't speak even a single word. For cleaning his hands and mouth after meal, he uses a *lota* not a jug. His hair is very long which falls to his thigh. He sleeps on a plank with a blanket made of sheep fleece not made in the factories of the multi-national companies. But in his office, he uses everything as he has to regard the constitution. But in his residence there is neither cooler nor television, neither refrigerator nor washing machine.... Obviously he is a redeemer. He is a true Hindu—a true devotee of Hinduism, the oldest religion of the world in which there were more than two dozen incarnations."

With the news there was a photograph of Sitaram which showed his style of eating and sitting.

According to a survey made by the P-TV, he was the most popular leader of the country and the people regarded him as man of *'Plain living and high thinking.'* Some people also believed that his look was seen even in water; and in the sky at night. Some also said that the manlike face in the moon was just like Sitaram.

The people also discussed his *dhoti-kurta,* moustache, stitching style of the clothes etc. They consider him as a leader of the *swadeshi movement* as he was the supporter of the handicraft.

On the other hand, the committee appointed by Sitaram submitted its report to the ministry.

"... reformation of IPC, reformation of police manual, no court fee for the people of the BPL, concession of fee for SC, ST and OBC, fast track courts, appointment of judges, mobiles courts, service of the retired judges, no political pressure on judges and on the judicial system, appointment of courts in rural areas, judge clubs and residences, handsome pay-scale for the judges, judges shouldn't participate in social, political, religious... programmes during their service period...," the committee recommended.

The report was submitted in seven hundred and eighty-one pages having different recommendations, "If the recommendations of the committee are implemented the corruption can be abolished, otherwise this curse on democracy will be settled strongly and democracy which is not only a system of rule but the greatest religion under which a human being is ruled and lives as a human being. This is no corruption, but a culture now. It is from bottom to top. None can deny it. It is not easy to get a man who is not corrupt if he has got such a chance. It is a sentiment of the people not an evil. It is second Nature. It is not easy to change it; only strong-will to abolish it can change it. None is safe. None can get justice except influential people. *Might is right* everywhere in India. Teachers from bottom to top don't perform their duties and they go to their working place to fulfil the quorum—to mention their attendance in their columns—to entertain and to perform their personal work. They also take French leave and get their salary illegally. The doctors in the government hospitals don't treat well without taking extra money. They run private nursing homes. Fake medicines are supplied in the hospitals. The market of medicine is full of fake medicines. The officers are committed to violate the rules as possible to the best of their knowledge and capacity. The same is the situation of *baboos....*"

The second part of the report was not too much critical and bitter; but its last paragraph was too bitter and factual as the people said.

"About seventy-five per cent of the government employees —gazetted and non-gazetted along with the teachers and the doctors are indeed no government servants but it seems that they've licence to defalcate money. For an example, there is a doctor who gets rupees four lac and fifty thousand per annum as salary but he doesn't work—he doesn't fulfil his duty and gets only salary illegally having taken French leave. Hence obviously it can be said that he misappropriated rupees four lac and fifty thousand as he had a licence as a doctor, Is it misappropriation? Is it no robbery? It is quite clear. Hence it can be said that seventy-five per cent of the government expenditure is misappropriated.... However the committee should never use such a language yet it uses only to show the fact—for the sake of the religion of democracy in the national interest—in the public interest as any kind of laxity regarding the corruption will be a major blunder...."

Sitaram promised the committee to table the report in the House during the next session and the people were hopeful about the implementation of the report.

CHAPTER

The Top Secret Meeting

The situation was too tense in Bhitta, a village in Bihar as the armed people of the RCC attacked the village and killed more than a hundred people and burnt their houses.

It was the month of May about 8 PM. In their attack except old men and ladies, all the inhabitants had been killed. The number of victims was one hundred and eighty-seven. They had been got stood in a row. They had their hands tied behind their backs with cable and finally with rope—all in one. They're gunned down together and they slept a final sleep. Their throats were cut and the armed group fled away with their heads. Their bodies were burnt, too. None was arrested. The police reached there the next night as the road was blocked with trees and landmines were set.

The politicians as well as the common people condemned the barbarous act of the RCC. Both the Houses of the parliament were boycotted by the Opposition leaders. They're anxious about the spread of Maoism in the country.

There was a great impact of RCC on fourteen states and they also instituted parallel government. The people of lower castes and the poor people of upper castes supported them.

There were also some other underground armed organizations all over the country, which paralysed the government system and snatched the lives of more than a thousand persons a year. Therefore, the central government and the state government treated it as problem of the national insecurity.

The central government was more anxious and appealed the armed organizations to surrender them with their arms and weapons. But they didn't do so and demanded the new governing system as the large number of population couldn't get social justice. Sitaram had to solve the problem as he was the Home Minister.

The chief of the army had already suggested the government not to deploy army in internal matters as they were no criminals but the extremists and it was not the matter of law and order; but they struggled to abolish evils like mismanagement, misgovernance, exploitation, social injustice, social inequality, suppression etc. They, therefore, became extremists for the sake of their own social rights—*bread, clothes* and *houses.* There was a great impact of the statement of the chief of the army on the public and on the government.The government agreed with the view and the common people welcomed his view. Therefore the all-party meeting was arranged and discussed different aspects of the issue in national and public interest. It was passed anonymously to begin a peace process through a dialogue.

With special reference to the meeting, the government held the top secret meeting and invited the extremist leaders. The Home Secretary participated in the meeting on behalf of the government and Krishna Munda on behalf of the extremist organizations.

In the meeting Krishna Munda said, "... even after half a century of independence eighty-five per cent of people have not got social justice. Most of them are schedule castes, schedule tribes, and other backward classes. They know nothing about law, democracy, constitution etc. They're unable to purchase even a single litre of kerosene oil. None comes to hear them. Their representatives don't want to take interest in solving their problems but take interest to enhance their own balance in their names. They defalcate the amount of the government treasury which is filled with the taxes of the common people—and submit bogus TA and DA bills. They also get forty per cent in commission of their quota and excite the officers of their own fields to do so and to pay them as political donation *i.e.,* political fees in the modern language. They're too corrupt and do everything wrong, possible by them; there are about one hundred and fifty MPs and one thousand seven hundred and ninety-five MLAs related to sex scandals. But in the eyes of democracy they are regarded as *bharat bhagya bidhata.* The same is the situation of the government employees, teachers, doctors, engineers, etc. As they join their posts, they bid farewell all the duties and remember only to get more and more salary, to get more and more commission, to defalcate and to exploit the common people. The government buildings of millions are weak but their private buildings of crores are strong. The former fall and the latter shine. Some take bribe... some steal tax. Some avail themselves of French leave... some defalcate government money. Some get commission and some purchase best things on paper and worst thing in reality. Some get illegal TA and DA. The percentage of the honest employees is about one per cent. This one per cent employees are harassed by the employees of their own departments. Only due to the corrupt political leaders and employees, not even a single government policy is successful on the ground but only on the papers. Therefore, all the government policies for development are paralysed. Hence, in spite of all the efforts made by the government—both the central and the states, there are the evils of poverty, starvation, illiteracy, spiritual and physical untouchablity, hypocrisy, bribery, partiality, sectarianism, conversion, extremism, injustice... everywhere in the country. None is safe in the country. The government has failed to provide education, houses, hygienic facilities for every citizen of India. Now the situation is too critical and most of the employees who've to do, don't go to the public to hear their problems; and deal themselves not as government servants but as monarchs. The teachers of the schools, colleges and universities also don't take interest in their own teaching work rather work out of their duties. Due to all this, the poor have been becoming poorer and the rich have been becoming richer. The condition of the labourers and the farmers is too critical and they're unable to buy even a packet of the iodized salt and a litre of kerosene oil. The latest items like; television, refrigerator, DVD, DTH, washing machine, air conditioner, air cooler, water filter etc are dreams for them—mystery for them. Democracy is an unsolving riddle for them—a mystery, too. On the other hand, the rich are passing their lives luxuriously and have proud to bring stars from the sky if necessary. The want to go to Mars to live. They never think to see the poor in happy state. The child labour is their own product and a business of their profit. So they never desire for the abolition of the evils. In spite of the government provision that it is a crime, more then two lac child-labourers are in Delhi only from Jharkhand; and they are sexually abused. They are socially, educationally, mentally, physically... exploited. They're treated brutally. Now it can be imagined easily. The poor are helpless for one kg salt or a pain-killer tablet but the rich claim for stars if necessary. Now it can be imagined very easily—what's the future of democracy. What is the future of democracy? What is the future of our country? Can the parliamentary democracy exist for a long time in such a situation in which some die of over eating and some are starved? Has the constitution or our democracy provided *Right to Equality* for each citizen, practically? Yes? We know. Are they living as human beings? No subsidy for the poor but undeclared subsidy for the rich. The farmer and the labourers commit suicide and the rich bake bread on their pyres. No? How many influential persons are convicted and penalised? Tell me? Any influential politician? Any capitalist? Any actor or actress? Any high-level officer? Yes? They're charged, I know it but at last they get clean chits. What is all this? Magic? It occurs in democracy? And it is tolerable in it? Bearable in it? Never... never... I say. Never! I'll wait no more. Either the government will have to provide social justice... or will have to listen to the voice of the guns. I'll wait no more! I say.... I'll blow all the government and the non-government factories, offices, institutions, police-posts and will loot the property otherwise, the government will have to listen to my *dukh-dard* (miseries and sorrows) – our problems.... None will be allowed to acquire the land of the poor in the name of development. If I die – we die, then I'll not let anyone live. I'll kill – we'll kill everyone. I think it is not wrong to say that I've killed – we've killed – our organizations have killed about twenty lac people during the last twenty years. I'm ready – we are ready – our organizations are ready to help the government to do anything in national interest – in public interest but the government will have to listen to our troubles. Otherwise the fire of our heart will burn all of you. No equality; no end of destructive or violent activities – as we're committed. If equality; end of violence. We are volcanoes...."

But the Home Secretary dismissed flatly all the grievances nursed by Krishna Munda.

"... do you forget that India is the greatest country in the world, where the power of the government resides in the public. After independence, the government has established hundreds of government industries, which are the modern temples of development. Don't you? You must know it. A number of scientific discoveries have been made in human interest and we get their advantage. Lacs of the educational institutions of higher education have been founded. There're more than hundred national highways. There are many engineering and medical colleges in the country which produce reputed engineers and doctors, who sacrifice their lives for the development of the country. There are no evils like; starvation, poverty, exploitation, suppression, bribery, rape, murder, social injustice etc. except a few cases; and who tries to take law in his own hand is convicted and penalized. All are equal. None is more equal or less equal. There is everywhere peace and rest—from Kanyakumari to Kashmir. There is the second place of Indian Railway in the world and very soon it may be placed in the first position. Each man under the *rojgar–guarantee scheme* gets employment under the different schemes—especially under the *Jawahar Rojgar Yojna*. Each and every village is connected with the main road. The brick-built houses are made instead of the mud built houses for the poor under the *Indira Awas Yojna*. Thousands of small and big canals have been dug for irrigation. As you know that India is known as a country for *unity in multiplicity* and the poor and the rich live together peacefully. There is social justice and social security and great spirit of love and brotherhood, too in the country. Fifteen per cent, seven and a half per cent and twenty-seven per cent seats are reserved for SC, ST, and OBC, respectively in government services under the *Social Justice Scheme*. The seats are also reserved in the educational institutions. This is the cause that now they live in the main current of the society. Two four-lane national highways have been built under the *Pradhanmantri Chaturbhuj Sadak Yojna*. The people of different religions, race, sect, caste, colour and ideology live together. There is the rule of law in the whole country. All the employees of the central government and the state government are public servants, whose religion is only service and who work only for the betterment of mankind. The politicians are public representatives, who work in public interest—the President, the Prime Minister, ministers, parliamentarians and legislators work in national and public interest. Teachers are very punctual and dutiful and they build the character of lacs of students every year...,' said the Home Secretary.

Listening to all this Krishna Munda got fired. Anyhow he was softened and expressed his reaction,"... tell me who are involved in several scams—*Boforce, Hawallah, Telecommunication, Fertilizer, MP-Quota, Bribe for asking question in parliament, Coffin, Tantasi-bhumi, Flood, Tehelka, St Keats...* ? Is a farmer involved?

Is a labourer involved? Are the poor involved? Who's involved? Do you know? Tell me? As they are elected as MPs or MLAs, they become millionaire within a month and they possess great buildings in the metros, a number of vehicles, possessors of costly plots, hectares of land, shoes of thousands, spectacles' frame of thousands.... From where? All this from where? Within a month from where? From the money plant or misappropriation? The bundles of notes in the parliament? In spite of all this, they can be regarded as public representatives or parasites who suck blood of the poor public. If they're public representatives, why do they get salary, allowance and pension, too as the government employees? They are public representatives but they misappropriate money. One can deal them as representatives but our organizations can never do this as *the wearer best knows where the shoe pinches.* Democracy weeps here—writhes here...."

The meeting was over without any decision till the next meeting, whose date would be decided later.

The Home Secretary communicated it to the Home Minister who suggested him to continue the peace process in future in the name of the next meeting.

12

CHAPTER

The Samadhan Commission

A new turn came into the political history of India when the *Samadhan Commission*, a five-member commission headed by Justice Shekhar Samadhan which was constituted by the previous central government, submitted its report to the government,The report was also known as the a-z formula.

The commission suggested, "...(*a*) dismissal of the parliamentarians and the legislators who've criminal record and restriction to contest any election in future—deprivation of the government welfare scheme—abolition of MP-quota and MLA-quota; (*b*) determination of educational qualification for the members of the parliament and the assembly by the High Level Commission headed by the judge of the Supreme Court; (*c*) dismissal of the corrupt bureaucrats; (*d*) dismissal of the employees who work on the different posts as officers, doctors, engineers, professors, teachers, clerks etc, who are corrupt; (*e*) deprivation of the government welfare scheme for those, who are corrupt; (*f*) their property must be seized by the government and must be declared as national property; (*g*) their prohibition to get any job in future related to the central government and the state government; (*h*) cancellation of their degree; (*i*) cancellation of their licence, which are related to the sensitive issue; (*j*) their conviction and punishment so that none could dare to do so in future; (*k*) publicity of their names in the gazette and in the newspapers—the names of the corrupt employees should be pasted into the notice boards of the government offices of their location; (*l*) award for the honest employees—their names and work should be published in the certain columns of newspapers; (*n*) provision of extra-ordinary promotion for those who work efficiently and eminently in their departments; (*o*) demotion for those employees, who degrade the department; (*p*) the constitution of the special courts for trial of the cases regarding corruption; (*q*) provision of ten per cent of reservation in the government services for the dependents of the honest employees; (*r*) appointment of spies to find out the issues of corruption; (*s*) after termination,compensation to their wards; (*t*) management of toll free telephone facility for complaints to help the government against corruption; (*u*) award for the person who informs about the corruption; (*v*) security of those who help the government against corruption; (*w*) a separate ministry for the abolition of corruption; (*x*) the constitution of the commission for awarding the persons related to it; (*y*) amendment to the police manual; and (*z*) amendment to the trial procedure...."

The report consists of one thousand one hundred and seventy-one pages which was submitted to the Home Ministry. It had two parts—the condition and the suggestion to the government. Without any further delay, the Home Ministry sent it to the Special Committee for reconsideration before tabling the report in the House. The special committee returned it to the ministry for tabling in the House with some necessary changes and the report was tabled in the next session for debate.

The debate was not unexpected. Whatever the public thought that happened there. Some members were its hard core supporters but some were against the report saying that—that was rubbish—the report of the frustrated mind but there was no fact—quite bogus and prejudiced to defame the country.

Biswas, who was a member of the House delivered, "... there is nothing in the report. Quite baseless and imaginary report of the great pessimist like Thomas Hardy, who has failed in his own private life and wants to give free vent to our country. The fact is just opposite. Just opposite. The employees, the bureaucrats and the leaders against whom he has raised question and question, work night and day in public interest. They've to work during the heavy rain or at midnight. There is no corruption-*forruption*. It is the product of his own mind. It is a rumour. Indian statesmen are regarded as the best representatives of the world. MP-quota is very-very important and necessary provision in Indian democracy and it must be continued. Only due to this there is all round development in the country. In this regard I keep keen interest and suggest the government to extend the quota—from two crore to fifteen crore. Rupees two crore to rupees fifteen crore! I also want to say on behalf of all the members of my party that if it is in India, there is no matter of anxiety as in this business—in this trade the money of the country remains in the country not goes out of the country...."

But the members who supported the report, boycotted Biswas' lecture. One of them was Deshraj, who strongly boycotted the lecture and delivered loudly, "nowadays the situation in the government offices is that not even a single piece of paper is moved without extra-money—without bribe and sometimes bride, too. Who doesn't participate in this exercise, his complaints are thrown into the dust-bin."

Meanwhile the members clapped loudly and said, "All's right—Quite right."

He continued, "It's not easy to get even a certificate without participating in the market of bribery. I think *if it were a rule to get a certificate to die, none could get it and would have died.* This is the current situation of our country. We say that there is democracy in India but the clerks say that there is *babooraj*. Others are not less than them. If one goes to the office, they roar not less than a lion rather more than a lion. Do you know, what do they say? Know it. They say, God, *too, is afraid of us—if God is unseen determiner of man, we are the seen determiners in this world*. They treat bribery as their religion. Now you can imagine if it is their religion what is the situation of the country. Who exercise this business are considered good, who don't are fools. Who get more bribe are the best. They explain and implement government rule in their own ways—in their own interest. The government buildings fall before inauguration and the private buildings seem as castles. How? From where? From the treasury of *Kuber*? No! Obviously! People know all this...."

But many members didn't agree with him and said, "This is the person who has got the report of this type submitted by Justice Shekhar Samadhan."

They opposed his lecture hardly and it seemed that then none could go forward to support his view. But fortunately some Anglo-Indian members stood up to participate in the debate and Deshraj began to narrate an event not fictitious but happened truly in Bihar and the media was highlighting the news:

> Shankar went to the passport office, Patna to submit the application, meanwhile Kamraj, a clerk was to the dealing window. Kamraj said to him to go to the window through an agent or to go the next day. So he went there through an agent. The agent requested him to accept the application on the same day. Firstly Kamraj expressed difficulty to do so, but when he requested him again and again, he demanded rupees two thousand. The agent gave him rupees fifteen hundred only and he accepted the application, but gave a receipt of rupees one thousand only. Getting the receipt of rupees one thousand only he claimed for rupees five hundred but he responded that rupees five hundred was his easy fee—his private fee and

if he wanted to get the passport in time, forgs the amount or he would have to exercise his feet and hands. Finally, he left the amount and went back to his home.

At home he waited for the passport for months but his desire was not fulfilled and he couldn't get the passport. Therefore, he contacted the agent to know the current situation and the agent told him that the application had been sent to the district police headquarter for verification. Knowing it he went to the district police headquarter to find out the situation but there he knew that his application had not been sent to the office.

Once again he went to the passport office, Patna and met Kamraj. Seeing him Kamraj asked him. "You've missed to sign the application at one column. I was waiting for you. OK. Very good. Fortunately you've come. Give rupees two hundred and sign here."

Shankar replied, "I've not brought money for you. I've money but for the fare only."

"You can go back WT (Without Ticket). Who asks for the ticket. You're a fool. Unnecessary expenditure for the ticket. Give me all the money. I keep keen interest in your work otherwise I can't say it. Whenever you come here you must keep Rs. 500-1000 in your pocket," said Kamraj.

Shankar gave all the money of his pocket and departed for his home.

Getting the money Kamraj also said to him to go back as it may begin to rain.

Reaching the railway station he took one seat in the express train. None asked him for the ticket but when the train was to stop soon at his home station, he jumped from the running train as he had no ticket and he was afraid of the TTE at the station. Misfortunately his right leg was fractured and was admitted to the government hospital where he passed more than a month.

As he had no ticket he was unable to claim for the compensation, legally. But knowing it one another passenger gave him his own ticket and said to show the ticket saying that someone had thrown him and he couldn't show the ticket because then he was nervous.

Getting the ticket he claimed for the compensation but the railway authority was not ready to do so. Getting the chance out of hand he promised the authority to give fifty per cent of the compensation in commission secretly. So the authority granted him rupees one lac. He signed all the papers needful but rupees forty thousand only was given to him.

"Rupees forty thousand only? This is the violation of the agreement. This is the great injustice."

"You don't know Shankar. You don't know. You've no practical knowledge. I've paid some other officers, too—from top to bottom. I've kept only rupees two thousand. Don't think. All this? I don't want to exploit you. I've pity for you so I helped you. Nothing new has happened. Everything happened according to the established traditions, which are implemented in all the government offices of India. I never want to violate the *established traditions*. Indeed this is the matter of our understanding."

Listening to all this Shankar okayed. He went back. After some days he went to the district police headquarter to know about the police verification and knew that until then the application for verification hadn't been reached there.

Knowing it Shankar put his hands on his head. The next day he went to Patna to meet Kamraj.

Seeing him Kamraj called him inward and said to him very slowly and friendly, "Heartily congratulation ! Once you're unable to purchase even a train ticket but now the Almighty God has given you rupees forty thousand, only because of my advice. God will give you something more in near future. I know. I'm also a future-teller. Perhaps you don't know. Let it go. I'll give you not only a passport but also a visa for Canada. You'll have many latest things; as—bungalow, car, refrigerator, computer, television.... What's not! Everything! Everything!"

"But until now you've not sent the file for verification."

"Don't worry."

"What? I don't get."

"I had disposed of the file on the very day but the head clerk had objected for your addresses."

"Sir, dispose of it very soon."

"Don't worry. I say. Listen to me whatever I say to you. Give rupees five hundred only to him. Only rupees five hundred so that he'll dispatch your file very soon."

"Sir I've already given you more than the real fee. But in spite of it now you demand more money."

"You're not a man of the age. You don't understand the matter. As he gets he will pass your application form soon. Rupees five hundred is not a heavy amount. Just now you've got rupees forty thousand."

Giving the easy-fee to the head clerk he went back to his home. He passed there two months but no news. So he went to Patna to meet Kamraj. Meeting him he began to speak angrily but Kamraj spoke not even a single word for five minutes and continued to listen to him.

Later he spoke, "Why're you angry with me. Now there is a new passport officer, who is honest and strict. There are different types of signature on the application, so he objected and therefore your file couldn't be sent. This is the fact but you continue to speak without knowing anything. Before speaking anything you should know the fact."

He was softened and signed the form. Signing he said to him, "Please send the file soon."

"This is the time of *omen*. You're the first client. The *bohini-batta* has not undergone. You should think about this."

Shankar considered the matter and he gave rupees eleven only to him.

"What is this? Which type of *bohini* is it? Is this the *dakshhina* of the *panditji*. Add one before the double one. Now you've no problem of money. Do you lack practical knowledge? You've to go to Canada so you must have practical knowledge. Only due to me you have got such a sum. Add one before the double one and give me. I'll get it heartily," said Kamraj.

So Shankar gave him rupees one hundred and eleven. One before double one! One, one and one!

Giving the money he became happy and on the way he dreamt, "... getting the passport I'll get a visa for Canada. I'll have a bungalow, a car...; and I'll come to India with a fair complexion after ten years. None in the village will parallel me. I'll marry a lady of Canada. The rest life with two wives—one from India and another from Canada—one in India, another in Canada. One wheatish and another white... full white. More time with the new.... But the villagers will be envious of me. Let them hate. I'll live in Canada if necessary."

After some days he went to the office of the Superintendent of Police and knew; till then no report—no file—nothing. He agitated himself and said, "I'll straighten him as a stick."

The next day he departed for Patna and met Kamraj at 4:00 PM.

Seeing the red face of Shankar he said, "Everything is well here. How're you? I was waiting for you and fortunately you've come. There is only one problem.The domicile certificate attached to the application has been issued by the second class gazetted officer but the new *Saheb* says to attach the certificate issued by the first class gazetted officer. Now the rule has been changed. Therefore, attach the new certificate to the application."

Shankar spoke nothing and as he turned to go back home Kamraj said to him, "O dear Shankar! I've a great mercy on you. Let me think for a minute....I think if you go there to bring another certificate, enough time will be taken and you'll have to expend much money. There is an option—one solution.

If you expend rupees five hundred only, you'll have not to wait for some days and within ten minutes your problem will be solved. One person can help you. I know about him."

"Who?"

"He remains far away from the client as he is VVIP. He doesn't perform this type of work but if I say to him, he'll do your work."

To whom shall I give the sum?"

"Don't worry. Give it to me and I'll give it to him."

So, he gave the sum to him and requested to dispose of the file soon.

But Kamraj did the same; and his file couldn't be disposed of by the office. The members of his family were annoyed with him and they said that he had undergone a cheater. Therefore, after some days he went to Patna agitatingly.

"*O bhai*! Shankarji! How are you? You are well? Tell me?"

"O Kamraj Baboo! It's not a petty mockery of me. I came here a number of times but yet there... problem... problem... new problem. You're cheating me. You've done enough. Enough! You've crossed the border. My leg was fractured only due to you."

Kamraj continued to listen to him but spoke nothing. As he became silent he began to describe the office culture.

"Why're you angry? You don't know about the office culture—about the offices of India? Where do you live? Do youn't live in India? This is the office of the government of India, not of my father. This is not my house and I've to deal everything. The head clerk has been retired. On behalf of him there is one another head clerk who touches the file after taking rupees five hundred as an easy fee. I'm a clerk not the head clerk and I've done my work regarding your application. Go to him and give rupees five hundred to him or give the sum to me I'll pay him. What you've to do, you've to say. Tell me. Tell me! Why're you silent? Just now you were roaring like a lion. It seemed that you're a lion and I was a goat. But now it seems that you're a squirrel. Who'll pay him rupees five hundred? I? Have you given the sum to me? Will I pay from my pocket. Why're you silent? Has your mouth been stitched?"

But Shankar spoke nothing and continued to listen to him helplessly.

"Sir! What should be done?" said Shankar after some moments.

"Listen to me only one thing—do you need the passport?"

"Yes."

"Indeed."

"Yes. Indeed."

"Now you're on the ground. It seems that you understand the office culture. If you want to learn more, listen to me silently."

He continued, "As the persons joins the government service he or she forgets everything except that he has to gain more and more. Anyhow. At any cost. None wants to touch the file without easy fee. So you must know that this office is also one of the government offices of India and we're the government employees. We're *baboos*. The *baboos* rule the office. Officers are ruled by us—we are not ruled by them. We're the engines. And do you not know the engines are run by diesel or petrol and diesel or petrol is purchased *bayee...* what? Not by the stone but by money. Do you know it? I'm not King Harishchandra—we are not King Harishchandra or don't want to be like him to starve. All people live under our rule—pass through us and we're the porters of Heaven. I think now you'll have known everything."

"I don't believe."

"You've to think yourself that you believe or not. But if you want to get the passport, give rupees five hundred to me and I'll pay it to him. If you want to get concession, for you rupees four hundred only. I'll request him on your behalf. You'll get the passport within two weeks. I know its solution. No tension of verification. I'll get done everything myself. If you want to get it within three days, you'll have to give rupees two thousand only."

"But I've rupees one thousand only."

"Don't worry. The rest amount will be expended by me. Later I'll get it from you. At present give Rs four hundred for the head clerk and rupees one thousand for others. I'm anxious about your passport as I love you very much."

Getting the sum he said once again, "*O bhai!* Come back very soon, as you pay the rest amount, the passport will be in your hand."

"I'll come back the next day to pay the dues—to pay *dews*."

Saying it Shankar went back to his home.

"OK.OK. No problem."

He met him the second day and paid the *dues*.

Getting the *dues* he said, "Tomorrow."

Listening to the word '*tomorrow*' he became very happy and said, "When... visa... for... Canada?"

"Very soon. Don't worry."

Tomorrow became *to-day*—the second day. Kamraj himself reached Shankar and said, "Have you got?"

"No."

"I sent the passport yesterday by *Super Post*."

"But I didn't."

"Perhaps due to the postal delay. You're very lucky as the person sitting beside me is an agent who has come to you from Bombay. He'll help you for getting the visa."

"Visa for Canada?"

"Yes. Yes. Aha! Visa for Canada!"

"How... ?"

"For others rupees forty thousand but for you rupees thirty thousand only. Rupees ten thousand concession for you. If you pay it today, rupees twenty-five thousand only for you and you'll get the visa within five or six days. I think the passport will also reach you tomorrow by mail. No more delay."

Continued after some time, "You're in my inner chamber of the heart. I can't forget you. Therefore, as the agent came to me I requested him on your behalf for the visa. The gentle man granted my request...."

Shankar became grateful, expressed debt of gratitude to them and gave rupees twenty-five thousand to Kamraj.

Getting it they went back. The passport also reached him the second day. He got the passport and informed Kamraj that he had got the passport.

He was very happy to secure success in the first stage of his mission to go to Canada. So he went to Patna to meet him and to pay debt of gratitude for the success.

As he met him, he opened the almirah, took out a visa and gave it to him.

"Take it. Go to Canada and give some amount at last to me (whatever you want). I'll say nothing about this. I've done everything for you. And now you have to do or to think. You've to decide yourself."

"Take it."

"How much?"

"Rupees one thousand only."

"I've no objection but you should think that only due to me you've got the passport and visa, too. I've to say nothing but you should give at least rupees five thousand to me. You should remember that you're going to be a millionaire within a year. You're going to join as an operator. Do you know what's its salary? Rupees one lac and ten thousand per month in Indian currency."

"Take rupees five thousand. Please give rupees two hundred only to me for fare."

"OK. Rupees two hundred for fare and rupees eleven for tea. Take rupees two hundred and eleven.... Enough for you."

Shankar went back and borrowed rupees one lac and ten thousand... from relatives for the fare of Canada and sold jewels of his wife, mother and grand-mother. He got the flight and reached Toranto. His passport and visa were verified there. They were found fake. Later he was sent to jail where he lost his temper. Once he tried to commit suicide by touching live wire. The members of his family starve in India....

The members heard this true event and nodded their heads. The debate was adjourned till the next day. Sitaram was listening to the event seriously.

13

CHAPTER

The Election

Unfortunately Sitaram fell into a critical situation as his cousin was arrested. The members of the parliament demanded his resignation and boycotted the house for several days. Hence, the Prime Minister said to him to resign but he didn't do so and the Opposition members continued to boycott for mounting the pressure on him.

They also demanded the debate of the issue and to postpone the debate of the a-z formula, but the government said that the issue would be discussed in the House just after the discussion of the debate of the a-z formula as the issue was relevant in national interest to abolish corruption from the country and the government was committed to do so at any cost.

There was an assembly election in his native state. Atmaram, who was the son of his father's sister was contesting for Gyanpur constituency. The election publicity was prohibited two days before the polling legally and none could do so.

The seat was too sensitive—politically and criminally. Police were deployed everywhere. The routes of the city were barricaded and the situation was watched seriously. The communication was under special sight of the police. Even the bicycle or bike was not allowed except the emergency services. The article 144 was imposed in the city and the administration was too alert and too tight.

It was the eve of the polling. The Gandhi-chowk seemed as the police cantonment. The police were holding flag marches. Meanwhile a *Bolero* vehicle passed. They indicated with hands to stop the vehicle, but the vehicle didn't stop. Hence, they overtook and the vehicle was stopped by them.

The police began to search the vehicle and interrogated the people in the vehicle. Atmaram came out and said angrily, "Do you not recognize me? I'm the brother of Sitaram—the brother of the Union Home Minister. I'll get your uniform taken off. Go away. I say to go away."

"Where're you going?"

"To send voter-lists."

"Is anything illegal in your vehicle?"

"No. Nothing. Only voter-lists."

"Only voter-lists?"

"Yes."

But the police suspected and searched the vehicle. During the interrogation it was noticed that the criminals of international level were sitting there with fifteen AK 47 rifles and four thousand bullets and bombs in a jute-bag along with rupees thirty-seven lac in cash.

So they asked him, "What's all this? Are these voter-lists?"

But Atmaram spoke nothing.

"Why do you carry all this? What's all this? Say to me. Why do you keep such a heavy amount? On the eve of the polling?"

"For welfare of the public?"

"Not to tempt the voters?"

"No."

"No. I say. No. Don't ask me more. Don't speak loudly. Where'll you live? Where will the members of your family live? Do youn't know Sitaram? I'm free. None can stop me from going anywhere. Ask someone else.... Not to me."

The police caught his hair and beat him too much. His both legs and hands were badly fractured. He was arrested and was sent to the police station.

The news was broadcast on radio and *Abhi Tak,* which was a popular TV channel. Knowing it Sitaram went to the police station with his hundreds of the supporters and got Atmaram released forcibly. Meanwhile, they were chanting:

End up, end up;

Police atrocity, end up.

Meanwhile, Sitaram was exciting the crowd saying, "This is the matter of my honour. Do or die."

The crowd attacked the police station and doors were broken. They also burnt the police station and the police vehicles. The police were also beaten and Atmaram was released by them forcibly; and the police were also beaten badly. Some of them were wounded, too.

All this was broadcast on *Abhi Tak* and other channels. People were happy to know that Atmaram was beaten and they treated him impartially as all were equal before law. They were excited to know that Sitaram and his supporters beat the police and the public; also burnt the vehicles and the station to get Atmaram released.

There was nothing in the name of law and order in Gyanpur for two days and the administration was totally paralysed. None of the administrative officers had courage to take action against them. The police also failed to command. Some of them were badly injured. Their rifles and bullets were snatched.

Three days passed. None registered even an FIR against Sitaram and others. Therefore, people criticized the state government. But on the other hand, the government expressed that police were not local, hence the FIR couldn't be registered and ordered the local station to register an FIR against the nameless persons.

Seeing the mockery of the democratic law, Sadhna, who was an advocate lodged a writ-petition in the High Court and demanded the registration of a fresh FIR against Sitaram and others; and Sitaram should be the main accused of the case.

"All the people know that Sitarm has got Atmaram released forcibly. He violated the law; and many rifles and bullets were looted by him and his supporters. The police station was burnt and the police were beaten, too. Some were injured. He has got a criminal released who had violated the code of conduct. Now it can be imagined that the person who violates the code of conduct has any right to participate in any democratic process. He is himself the Union Home Minister. Being the Union Home Minister he took the law in his hand. Can he be regarded the Union Home Minister of democratic India—of the world's largest and greatest democratic country. He has committed a heinous crime against democracy and the state government tried to save him. The role of the local administration was partial. Millions of Indians were watching their own televisions. Seeing it there is a lack of faith in democracy. The people think that if the police is not safe in the country, who is safe. How the public are safe here The politicians are regarded as the watchmen of democracy, but it seems that they don't bear such a character. If they don't honour the law, will the common people honour it ? Is there any chance ? No chance. In such type of cases none should be allowed to take law in his or her hand for the sake of law, constitution, and democracy....I, therefore, beg to issue an order to the state government to register an FIR against Sitaram, Atmaram and others," said Sadhna.

Getting the matter in public interest the High Court delivered its judgement, "... this is the matter in public interest—a heinous crime against law, constitution and democracy. All are equal before law and even an influential person can't go out of the law. Hence the court orders the state government to register an FIR against Sitaram, Atmaram and others for the sake of law, constitution and democracy."

In this regard the local police station registered the FIR against them. Sitaram was the main accused in the case and most of his relatives were co-accused. The police took hard step to arrest them. The accused were arrested on the same day but Sitaram and Atmaram were not arrested. So, the police raided several places of Sitaram and Atmaram but couldn't get success. None was present in the houses of Sitaram and Atmaram except some servants.

The people were very pleased with the historical judgement of the High Court and with the police action to arrest them.

They once again began to believe, "... law is supreme and none can go out of it. The catchment of law is very strong. Even a millionaire can not take law in his or her hand. We're ruled by the law of the democratic constitution not by a person or persons...."

On the other hand, the politicians as well as the public continued to criticise Sitaram and the role of the Central Government. They demanded Sitaram's dismissal. The members of the parliament boycotted the session to mount pressure on the government for his dismissal but the government didn't desire to dismiss him as there was fear of the withdrawal of his support. But in spite of all this, the Prime Minister was compelled to do so and suggested him to resign the post.

Sitaram didn't resign the post and began to ill-fame the state government and the media, too.

He wrote a letter to a correspondent, "... the judgement of the court is not impartial and same is the condition of the media. They want to gloom my popularity. I was not involved in the illegal activities which took place in Gyanpur. When it happened I was admitted to the hospital in New Delhi as I was seriously ill. Perhaps my photograph has been mixed with the crowd with the help of the computer by the TV channels. My voice may be mixed. Everything is possible in this age of computer. It is out of imagination that I can commit such an evil. Heh! I can't do this. This is a heinous crime against democracy. There is one another fact that the objectionable things like rupees thirty-seven lac, rifles and bullets were not in the vehicles but they were kept by the police and the leaders of the opposition parties to defame Atmaram. He knew nothing about all that, as he was a gentle man and the most popular leader of the state. People hold him on their *palms and hands*. The result of the election will prove that how popular he is. The day of the counting will be the day of Atmaram. I've firm faith and blind belief in law and constitution and God, too. I'll gain justice in future and I'll not resign the post. If I resign the post, it will come as a shock for the poor—for helpless people. I say I'll not resign and will continue to execute my duties."

This letter was published in most of the daily newspapers.

Reading the letter in the newspapers people reacted, "... hundred per cent liar. Heh! Heh Sitaram! Heh you must die! Have you no shame? Non-bailable warrant against you, but no shame to resign from the cabinet. Our PM is also mute and dumb as he doesn't demand your resignation. He also helps you only for the sake of the government not for the sake of democracy."

Due to this reaction, the Prime Minister again suggested him to resign the post just then.

Getting the hard decision and suggestion to him he resigned.

"... I resign from the cabinet according to the voice coming from the inner chamber of the heart."

Getting his resignation, the Prime Minister took the breath of relief and sent his resignation to the President, and he accepted his resignation.

As he resigned he began to try for his bail—firstly in the Lower Court and secondly in the High Court; and in the High Court his bail was granted. So he distributed the quintal of sweets and there was no shame.

Only a week had passed that he once again got the ministry—the Home Ministry. But when he was taking vow the Opposition leaders as well as the common people were unhappy and they were criticizing him and the government.

"He is a blotted minister. Therefore, we'll not ask him any question in the House or we'll not listen to him," the opposition leaders said.

But Sitaram's reaction was harder than that of politicians.

He said, "I'm a minister in national interest not in members' interest. I've to serve *Bharatmata* not them...."

The Special Commission was constituted by the Supreme Court to investigate all the cases of Sitaram and others for the quick disposal of all the issues. Hence, the commission demanded the files related to him and they were submitted to it. Just after some days it was noticed that on the occasion of the Holi festival the office was closed and at night fire broke out; and all the files of the cases were burnt.

The next day, this news was published in most of the daily newspapers.

When Sitaram knew that all the files of his cases had been burnt he reacted, "... I wanted to face the trial in the court of law as I believe in law, so that the public might be aware of *dudh ka dudh ; pani ka pani*. But oh! God has snatched the golden chance. *God shines even in fire....*"

As all the files were burnt and there was no record to prosecute him hence the commission was terminated by the court.

The people said that the files had been burnt not misfortunately but perhaps by Sitaram's worldly formula to save himself.

The Opposition leaders demanded reframing the charges against him and to investigate the causes of the fire but the government said that in lack of evidence the charges couldn't be reframed as it would be an excess for him.

In spite of heavy pressure, the government didn't take legal action for reframing and to find out the cause of the fire.

The Sword on Corruption

Deshraj and some other members of the house mounted pressure on the government, so the Special Session of the parliament was called on to discuss the debate of the a-z formula. After the debate of full a week the votes were cast. The report of the *Samadhan Commission* was passed and became law to abolish corruption.

There was a mixed reaction to the historical decision of the parliament. There was a violent uproar all over the country. The public were happy with the law, but the Opposition leaders and the government servants were too sad.

Some opposition leaders said that the law had been implemented only to crush the opposition leaders; and the employees said that that was the violation of the rights of the government servants and others.

The reaction of the government servants was too hard and considerable:

> "... there is nothing in the name of corruption. The government had misunderstood the matter. The lives of lacs of people will be destroyed because of this law. This is an established system, no corruption. It is not harmful

even for the country as in this *trade*, money of the country remains in the country. Indeed it is a *market*—it is *trade* of rupees three hundred and fifty crore per annum. Three hundred and fifty-one per cent of the national budget. Indeed it is *trade*; and ninety-nine per cent politicians and employees participate in this official culture honestly and punctually. Only due to this *trade* the great buildings of the politicians and the employees are visible; the clerk may become a millionaire, otherwise nothing can be done with the help of salary. Salary is nothing for us; our everything is the *trade* which can't be forbidden. We're ready to die but not to leave the *trade*. This is India—*Mother India*. We've fundamental rights to enjoy Indian environment. The commission has failed to study the fact—the fact is that only due to this *trade* the GDP of India has increased; and India is the largest country in the world in consuming the products of the national and multi-national companies; and none in India has capability to purchase their things except who participate in the *trade*. The government doesn't know that the farmers who plough hectares of land are incapable to purchase more than *salt* and *oil*. It can be imagined easily. If we don't, who'll purchase the things produced by the companies. None. They'll be locked. There will be unemployment and the common people will die of starvation. The same will be situation of the hundred per cent salaried employees.... Hence, the government should never forbid us to do so in public interest—in national interest. They are the real criminals, who want to spoil the *trade*. We're not criminals. Here the matter differs. Whatever we gain that is by fate or by chance. The *give and take* system is not an evil—not a bribe as it is *given and taken* spiritually. To hurt anyone is a crime, but in the *trade* we don't hurt anyone. This trade is done under the principles of '*may all be happy*' and '*may all prosper*'. There is nothing wrong in it. While giving and taking we follow the ethics. This is one of the important parts of the office culture. So, this is not a matter of anxiety and the government should encourage this holy system."

Most of the politicians were also more or less against the law to abolish corruption. One hundred and thirty-nine cases were lodged against the new law in different courts by the different non-employees and employees' organisations. Most of the cases were lodged by the organisations of North India; especially of Bihar and UP. Not even a single case was lodged by labourers and farmers.

The employees' organisations also criticized Sitaram as he played important role for the implementation of the report of the *Samadhan Commission*. Hundreds of his effigies were burnt, but as the Union Home Minister he tried to crush the movements against the law and he had become the thorn of the eyes of the employees; and of some politicians. They went on strikes, boycotted the government programmes, and burnt a number of railway stations, trains and buses.

Considering the matter seriously, the Supreme Court took an immediate step and issued an order to transfer all the cases instituting in the different courts to the Supreme Court within twenty-four hours. All the cases were transferred and the court issued a stay-order till the disposal of the case.

The trial began which took three years and after the long trial the court delivered its judgement.

"... the law is historical in national and public interest. Its motive is to abolish corruption and to provide neat and clean administration.... Hence all the cases lodged against the report of the *Samadhan Commission* (a–z formula) are dismissed...."

The complainants as well as employees and politicians were shocked at the decision of the court. They criticized the court for such a decision and boycotted the work of the government. There were many violent clashes. The property of the government was destroyed. The work in the government offices was stopped. Seeing the violent out of control, Sitaram resigned the post.

But the rule remained implemented. Hundreds of the politicians were forbidden to contest any election and were arrested. Lacs of employees were dismissed and were prosecuted. Their property was seized and was declared as national property...."

The media cast this type of news in special columns and the people read it eagerly.

On the other hand, there was an atmosphere of deep distress in the houses of the corrupt employees and they arranged processions with a slogan usually:

Sitaram; *haay-haay,*

Sitaram; *murdabad-murdabad.*

Central Government; *murdabad-murdabad.*

In those days the work in the government offices was easily done. No demand. No bribe. No delay. No leave. No fever. No fret. No absentee. Nothing unwell. Everything well. Everything properly. Everything on schedule. Nothing out of the schedule. Never weariness. Never....

The public said that if the rule remained implemented for ten years only, India would become a golden bird—Elizabethan England—Ashoka's India—Samundragupta India—a dream of Gandhi—the most developed country of the world.

There was a very good atmosphere in educational institutions. The teachers were punctual. They took responsibility for the students; and their guardians were in regular contact with the teachers. The same was the situation in the hospitals. The doctors performed their duties sincerely. The service to patient became their religion.

The leaders of the opposition parties criticized the government saying that only the leaders of the opposition parties were crushed by the law and the leaders of the ruling parties were not the victims of the law. Hence, they demanded the resignation of the Central Government; and for mounting pressure they boycotted the parliament. They were still unmoved to their demand for resignation.

Getting the situation critical, the government resigned and the President accepted its resignation but the *Lok Sabha* hadn't been dissolved. No front was capable to form the new government and none wanted to go before the public to get a verdict. They, therefore, began to form new alliances but when they failed to do so they made effort to form the national government, but it, too, failed. It seemed that the country was going to face the Parliamentary By-Election.

The President also took interest to constitute the government in national interest but he failed to do so.

But a sudden turn came into Indian Politics that a new alliance came to light having the proper number for majority in the House and Sitaram was elected as leader of the alliance.

Sitaram claimed to form the government and the President invited him to take vow. The 157-member council of ministers took vow.

"Democracy is the government of fools. The party of three members has formed the government and the single largest party supports the government. This is the excess committed against democracy. This is the mockery of it. They're enjoying in the name of it. Sitaram's father who was an ex-jemindar, he had tons of gold and silver, who had spent it to get the support of MPs...," the people said.

Only one week had passed that the INC(P) which supported the government withdrew its support and the government lost the vote of confidence in the House. Hence Sitaram with the council of ministers resigned; and he could hold the post of the Prime Minister only for seven days.

This political crisis jerked democracy and the constitution. The intellectual persons as well as the common people criticized such a role of the political parties. So, the President himself called the all-party meeting and suggested them to choose their leader in the House, but they didn't do so. As the second option he suggested the INC (P), the single largest party to choose a new leader which chose Deshraj as a leader.

Therefore the President invited him to take vow, and Deshraj took vow along with the 27-member council of ministers; Sitaram was also present there. The government got the vote of confidence within five days.

During the next session of the House some members once again demanded reframing the charges against Sitaram.The government accepted their demand and a five-member judicial commission was constituted to do so, which had to submit its report within forty-five days.

The common people were very happy. Deshraj was a popular leader who was famous for *Gandhism*, simplicity, honesty, sincerity.... Seeing his simplicity, some people mocked him.

Sitaram was the first person after the President, who expressed congratulation to him; and he desired for merging the New Welfare Party into the INC (P).

The a-z formula remained implemented. The result was that about thirty-three per cent of the employees were either suspended or terminated; and forty per cent of the employees were facing trials under the different charges against them.

The whole administrative system seemed changed. Nothing old—everything new. The situation was that the percentage of crime fell to the rate below 1952s crime rate. Merely a case of rape, murder, robbery, clash, riot etc was heard in the interval of months. It seemed that not only the people but the dust also knew that that was the rule of democracy—the rule of law. No tension. No despair. No escapism. No isolation. Only happiness. Happiness and happiness.

In the meantime, the *five-member judicial commission* submitted its report in which charges against Sitaram had been reframed.

Once again the news attracted the attention of the public and they were happy expecting that Sitaram would be definitely prosecuted and penalized by the court. But this news was the second important news for the public and the first priority was to the news related to the action against corruption. The government distributed prizes to those who informed secretly about the corrupt government employees and about crimes too. Lacs of people were awarded prizes. Many employees as well as teachers were also awarded prizes for good performance. It seemed that the people lived in the Classical Age.

Then the turn had been changed. Deshraj was the most popular leader in the country. The people praised him too much.

"... now it is obvious that we live in democracy, We're free. Under the constitution—not under the person or pressure. If such condition remains continued for ten years, we've no poor man in India. Before this, most of them continued to misappropriate government funds and corruption was everywhere in India—the corruption was the pulse of India. But with Deshraj the situation is fully changed. He is the son of a grazer who knows the ground reality. He'll definitely abolish corruption from India. It is the main evil of India. As it ends, ninety-nine per cent evils of India will be abolished automatically. He was born in a shed and now rules the world's largest democratic country. The media is partial as it doesn't cast the news related to him. On the other hand, the news related to Sitaram was cast usually by the media. Deshraj is a true *Gandhist* and Sitaram is too corrupt who misappropriated crores of rupees in the state while he was the Development Minister and the Chief Minister of the state; he has got an MLA killed; he has got the files burnt; he has got his cousin released illegally. But on the other hand no pomp no show by Deshraj and has become the Prime Minister of India—*our* Prime Minister. Now it is quite obvious that a shed born man can occupy the highest post. Now it is said that Sitaram continued to enjoy call girls in the five star hotels and showed himself as a *balbrahmchari....*"

Suddenly a new turn came into Indian politics when the earthquake caused damage to property in Kashmir and the central government focused its attention on Kashmir. Deshraj's keen interest came as great relief for the earthquake victims. The result was that the people of Pakistan occupied Kashmir reviewed their stand.

There was a new turn in the life of Abdul. He lived in Punchh. The earthquake snatched the lives of thousands of the people. Many people lost their near and dear. There was also the loss of the property of millions in Punchh and some other areas. Indian army played the most important role to give relief to the victims after the earthquake. They served them as their blood relatives. Some dead bodies were recovered from the fallen houses. Some remained pressed in the ruined houses and their relatives didn't see even their dead bodies. Many wounded persons were admitted to the hospitals.

Abdul was living in a relief camp provided by the government as his house was badly damaged by the earthquake. He had lost all the members of his family. He himself was badly wounded.

As Abdul became well he decided to fulfil the uphill task which was hunting his heart for thirty days. He wanted to meet his paternal uncle, aunt and their children who lived at Midur in Muzzafarabad of Pakistan occupied Kashmir.

He was quite unaware of them. Either they saved themselves from the cruel hand of the earthquake or passed away. This was hunting his heart. He was unable to go there as the border between India and Pakistan was sealed. When the governments of India and Pakistan decided to open the border of the Kisanganga sector after some days he also reached there to cross the border to meet her blood relatives or to know their condition. He waited there for five hours with the people assembled there, but he was not allowed to cross the border.

Although he was forbidden to cross the border, he was determined to go there. He, therefore, didn't come back to the camp in Punchh and began to live in one another relief camp near the border line.

There were many people who had been affected by the earthquake. Therefore, Abdul served the earthquake victims for fifteen days in the camp. And after fifteen days the border was opened once again; he was allowed to cross it. Having crossed the border he moved on foot as the vehicles were not plying on the road and the road was broken and jammed, too, with the snow rocks. After eight hours of his step march he reached Midur and saw that the house of his relatives was ruined by the earthquake. None of them was present there. When he didn't get them there, he went to the hospital which was run in a camp by the doctors of the Indian Army. There he searched each and every bed and got Roshani, his cousin who was badly wounded. Her both legs and both hands were wounded. Seeing Abdul Roshani said, "... except me all the members of my family passed away." Knowing it he began to weep, sat on her bed and communicated his message.

Seeing the miserable condition of Roshani he decided to stay there to serve her. He lived there for one and a half months. After the medical treatment in the *Aman Hospital* founded by India in a camp and his true service to her she became well and was discharged from there. Hence she got well soon and began to live with Abdul in a relief camp of the village.

But Abdul decided not to come back into Punchh as he had already lost everything in Punchh. The government offered Rs 40,000 as a grant to each victim to built a new house, but she denied to do so and said, "... Kashmir is my house."

Once Abdul said to Roshani very emotionally, "... we have lost everything except *'I'... 'you' and 'you'... 'me'*. Our fate has already been determined by the Almighty. We have been assembled here by God; not physically only but spiritually, too. Hence we should embrace one another socially...."

Roshani became ready and said to him, "OK! I'm agree with you. Yes! our fate has been determined by the Almighty. We should definitely follow Him; the Supreme Order...."

They communicated their decision to the neighbours. Therefore, they agreed with them and arranged a marriage ceremony. They were married socially. After the marriage, they decided to serve the earthquake victims. They, therefore, usually visited the victims and served them. They also collected money as a donation and distributed it among them. Where'er and whenever they went for it, some people wanted to know about them and they introduced themselves as *Roshani of Pakistan occupied Kashmir and Abdul of Indian Kashmir.* Knowing it people wondered and said, "... no border... no control line... no limitation... only love... only brotherhood... only virtue... they serve the earthquake victims... they collect donation from the public to serve the victims."

There was a matter of the common discussion all over Pakistan that in spite of Pakistan's support for terrorism in Kashmir, India was playing the most important role to serve the earthquake victims in Pakistan; and there was a great impact on the common people. Deshraj became popular in the earthquake affected area of Pakistan, too.

Once it happened that Abdul and Roshani visited a tea stall. Salim and Shaif were taking tea there. In the meantime, Salim said to Shaif, "... Shaif! You can imagine what India is. What's India? India is a true neighbour of Pakistan. India donated Rs 850 million to Pakistan to serve the victims. Deshraj himself takes keen interest in the relief work for the victims. He himself wanted to visit here. There was one another proposal of India to send some helicopters in Pakistan to serve them, but Pakistan denied and as a result a number of Pakistanis lost their lives. We live here as slaves... as mojahids... not as human beings."

Shaif was agree with him. His reaction was harder than that of Salim. He said, "You're right! Quite right! Who live in

India are free and fearless. The government takes immediate step for them if they meet any kind of casualty! Muslims are treated as true human beings in India; but on the other hand, some Muslims in Pakistan are treated as mojahids. Pakistan occupied Kashmir is in national interest of Pakistan not in our own interest; and the *MacMahon Darra* has been given to China. This is the proper moment to think – we should live in Pakistan or in India? Definitely, we should live in India never in Pakistan; and *Kashmir Never in Pakistan....*"

All this was heard by Abdul and Roshani. They wondered. The dialogue between Salim and Saif awarded a new way to them (Abdul and Roshani). They, therefore, began a mass movement for change – *Kashmir Never in Pakistan*. Firstly, they arranged a programme in Muzzafarabad. Thousands of people participated in it. The meeting was addressed by them.

Roshani delivered, "... do you know?... the most proper time to end the atmosphere of fear and terror, bloodshed and violence, murder and rape, intolerance and extremism from Kashmir and to get the isolated part attached to India. India is a peace loving country; on the other hand, Pakistan's fundamental duty is to support terrorism to kill our own brothers – our own sisters and to destroy the property of our own.... Pakistan supports terrorism, extremism and all the evils under the sun as possible. We should know it. We should support India and we should ignore the bad intention of Pakistan. There is no partiality in India; and Hindus and Muslims live together peacefully. India is a secular country of the world. There is nothing in the name of democracy in Pakistan and India is the largest democratic country in the world. There is all round development in India but in Pakistan there is the development of barbarism, terrorism, extremism... against the mojahids, minorities and innocent people."

"... all's right! I welcome all this heartily. The programme is the lighthouse and it will enlighten whole Kashmir. Kashmir is the place, where the beautiful girls with the natural beauty take birth. Not only physical beauty but also spiritual beauty.

The message of the spiritual beauty is peace and rest in Kashmir—in India. I promise... we promise... our beauty... our spiritual beauty promise.... This is the only demand of the present time...."

Listening to her, the public began to chant:

Inqlab-Jindabad.

Integrated Kashmir'Jindabad'

Bharatmata 'Jindabad'

Gokhale-Tilak 'Jindabad'

Gandhi-Bose 'Jindabad'

Abul Kalam, 'Jindabad'

Bhagat-Azad, 'Jindabad'

The hearts of the common people swelled with the new hopes and confidence—with the sense of peace and rest; for the development of Kashmir and desire to live as a man.

Knowing it, the leaders of the Pakistan occupied Kashmir became very glad. They arranged a meeting of the political and religious leaders. In it they moved a resolution having twenty articles entitled *'Kashmir Never in Pakistan.'* It was passed anonymously.

The central government was very very pleased with the stand. The common people were also very happy and they whole-heartedly supported the stand of the government and the people of the Pakistan occupied Kashmir. The government handled the issue very seriously and cautiously.

People said, "Deshraj is a great patriot. He tackled the event of the earthquake in such a way that a new ray of hope came across the border. Very soon Pakistan occupied Kashmir will become the part of India once again. All this is possible only because of Deshraj."

15

CHAPTER

Law is Supreme in Democracy

The government lodged a case against Sitaram in the Special Court of the High Court—the court in which many cases were instituted against many influential persons.

On the other hand, the leaders of the opposition parties criticized the government saying that it suppressed the opposition leaders knowingly and Sitaram had become the victim of bad intentions of the government. They said that all the charges against him were prejudiced and baseless only to blur Sitaram's honour in politics; and he had become the victim of political conspiracy.

"Sitaram is an honest person. Only to defame him and to get him turned from the Indian politics. He is the messiah of the poor—of the downtrodden people. None can imagine that he has committed such crimes. He has become the victim of political conspiracy. The charges against him are baseless and prejudiced so they must be withdrawn. It will be in national interest—in public interest...,"said the leaders of the opposition parties.

Although the court issued a notice to him and the trial began; and they continued to criticize the government—

.especially Deshraj, then Prime Minister. His case was at the top of the list of hearing. Sadhna and Shamim were counsels for the prosecution and the defence, respectively.

At her youthful stage, Sadhna expressed her desire to marry Sitaram but he refused to do so saying that he had to serve the country; and the marriage would be a chain for him. So, he couldn't marry her. Due to this Sadhna had taken a vow to remain a spinster and did so.

But when she was nominated as a counsel for the prosecution, he himself requested her secretly to marry so that she could help him during the trial. He wrote a letter secretly:

> "*All is well that ends well.* The world knows this. Those days I couldn't accept your proposal which was a blunder for me and for that blunder I express deep distress. Please pardon me. If you do so—O! my queen if you do so it will be the greatest mercy on me and the poor. I think I'm not your hero socially but I'm in your heart definitely until now. I passed the most part of my life in public service but now none wants to hear me. I've firm faith and blind belief that in such a situation you'll protect me to the best of your knowledge and capacity. I'm too sorry to say that in spite of your deep love for me at the young age, I forgot you. Please pardon me.... Now I'm in the most critical situation of life and none wants to contact. I know your heart is softer than cotton and only one wave of your heart will prove me innocent in the court. You'll be very very pleased to know that I welcome you and request you to marry me—to marry the former Prime Minister of India, secretly; and it will be disclosed just after the disposal of the case.... I request you not to disclose it to anyone....With regards... coming from the inner chamber of the heart....Yours lovingly... Sitaram...."

"You've attempted to dynamite democracy and the constitution; the constitution which has awarded justice to the citizens of India. Each and every citizen has a duty to defend its existence and honour. National interest is above anyone's interest. Even God can't save you, can't help you. I can't cheat the Almighty, the constitution, the law...." Sadhna sent an SMS.

On the other hand the trial continued.

"... The accused held several posts and misused his posts and power. He misappropriated the government fund in his own interest. Crores of rupees have been misappropriated by him when he was the Development Minister in the state. He got the files burnt with the help of the criminals only to save himself from the impartial hand of justice.... I, therefore, beg you to prosecute Sitaram under different sections.... If any kind of laxity for such crimes is given, it will be a mockery of democracy. The accused has plotted to dynamite our democracy. I beg the court to take a very stern and inexorable view of the accused's crime without being trapped in any sentiment...,"said Sadhna in the court.

But Shamim, the counsel for the defence, cross-examined all the charges and said, "... my client is quite innocent and has become the victim of political malice and plot. He executed his duties honestly and impartially. He is one of the *Gandhists* of India and has never misappropriated any kind of property in his life. He is famous for honesty and simplicity. He is the only Prime Minister in the history of independent India, who executed his duties honestly. According to the plebiscite of a private TV channel he is the most popular leader in India. He is the messiah of the downtrodden people and he can never go against law. The charges which have been reframed against him are prejudiced and baseless. Quite illusive and imaginary. He is *Gandhist*, dutiful, honest.... I, therefore, beg you to dismiss all the charges against him for the sake of humanity and constitution...."

Meanwhile, a new issue came to the country. The Supreme Court delivered a judgement against a Kashmiri terrorist supported by Pakistan for killing eighty-one persons and sentenced him.... But some people began to demand his clemency in national interest so that the peace-process between both the countries could remain continued. This was the matter of debate all over the country. Regarding this editorials and articles were published in the newspapers usually.

The accused lodged an appeal before the President for clemency. Some political parties, social organizations, human-right organizations, writers and intellectuals were in favour of his clemency but some were against the clemency, too.

Some organizations requested the President for his clemency and he changed the decision of the court in national interest. But some other organizations criticized the decision of the President and it was opposed all over the country.

So, the Supreme Court took the issue seriously and demanded the case for reconsideration under sections.... of the Indian constitution.

On the other hand, the trial of Sitaram was finished and was prosecuted under sections...."

It was Saturday. The day of the decision of the case—the day of the decision of his fate. He stood in the accused-box. None was with him except his counsel. His look was sad. It doesn't seem that he was once the Prime Minister. None for him. None with him. His duty only. Duties were not ready to leave him.

"... the court studied all the parts of the case of both sides seriously and came to the conclusion that Sitaram was guilty—had misused the power of the posts. If he is allowed to do so even God can't save this democratic country. He usually took law in his hand; and he forgot that every citizen comes under the catchment of law. Law is supreme in democracy. None is above it. Nobody can violate the order of law and the constitution.... In regard of the law and the constitution he is found guilty under sections.... Hence, the court passes prison sentence...."

16

CHAPTER

Sitaram and His Realization

An appeal was lodged by Sitaram in the Supreme Court against the judgement of the High Court. The appeal was admitted. Hence the bail-petition was filed by Sitaram. His bail-petition was granted and he was released from the jail.

Having come out from the jail, he moved to metaphysics. He usually passed maximum time to worship gods and deities. He visited a number of temples or *majars* daily. In the first week of his move to metaphysics he visited at least one hundred temples or *majars* of the *Sufi* saints.

There he usually said, "O Almighty! Save me! Protect me! I'm in the most critical situation of life. In such a critical situation only you can save me—protect me, otherwise...."

He usually visited Swami Maharaj, who was his religious *guru*. In the *ashram* of the *guru* he requested him to bless him to be free from problems. And Swami Maharaj said to him, "You've become the prey of the fury of Saturn. Continue to drop water and jaggery in the root of the *peepal* tree on each Saturday and soon you'll be free from the bad effect of Saturn. There will be no problem. Also wear a finger ring of the iron made from the horse-shoe of the black horse. It'll also help you to be free from the bad effect of Saturn.

Knowing about the solution suggested by Swami Maharaj, Sitaram felt secured. He was very very hopeful about for the solution and very happily he began to perform the ritual suggested by Swami Maharaj.

But in spite of all this he was fallen into illusion. Therefore, he usually posed so many questions before Swami Maharaj. Hence he was anxious about the doubtful situation of his own follower.

Oneday he was totally nervous, fell flatly on his feet and began to ask him many questions. He answered all the questions for hours and the discussion was published in the *Ashram Sandesh,* which was a weekly magazine of the *ashram:*

"O Maharaji! What's the total meaning of life?"

"The total meaning of LIFE is *'living interpretation of fact for ever'* where L = living, I = interpretation, F = fact and E = ever. It means to say that life is a force which should perform only virtuous work as possible. Life is a God-gift. So, the gift should be kept virtually. Only a godly man gets salvation otherwise...."

"What's the characteristic of life?"

"Virtue is the characteristic of life. Virtue means life. No virtue, no life. It is said that immortality lies in virtue. Only human virtues establish man as a man otherwise man is also like animal, naturally."

"Which is the meanest being in this universe? Someone says that man is the meanest being in this universe. Is man the meanest being?"

"Man is the meanest being in this universe and also the best being. Evils of man establish man like the meanest being *e.g.;* sinful acts in Nithari. Virtues of man establish man like the best being as; welfare schemes of Indian Army in earthquake affected areas of Kashmir. Only virtue separates man from the other beings."

"Is man perfect?"

"No! Except God, none is perfect in this cosmos."

"Should man be omnivorous?"

"Never! Man should be always vegetarian. The Almighty has given us various kinds of fruits, grains, nuts, etc to eat. They are available in Nature. He should follow the religion of non-violence. All beings are equal in regard of life. Life is dear for each being. If man is the best being in the cosmos, man should bear this responsibility."

"What's the way of life?"

"The way of life is truth and non-violence."

"If we follow all this in our life, what will be got?"

"You'll get everything. There will be no physical gain but spiritual gain. Man should do everything for the satisfaction of his spirit not of his body as spirit is immortal and body is mortal. Man should prefer the demand of the spirit not of the body. We should prefer spiritual gain to physical gain."

"But I see that the persons who choose virtuous path suffer—the world compels them to suffer. And if man commits evils, he also suffers. Sometimes it happens that who commits evils doesn't suffer and who prospers to virtue, suffers. Why does it happen? Is there any role of chance in life?"

"They attain physical prosperity not spiritual prosperity. Which is meaningless. Spirit is fact and body is an illusion—Spirit is true and body is false. The meaning of physical prosperity is meaninglessness. And who prosper spiritually are in contact with Divine Light—the light through which man joins God's empire—enters God's empire, which is far far away from the reach of physical prosperity. Chance also plays important role in life but only for the physical gain. There is no role of chance in spiritual life."

"It means?"

"Man should always lead a life of virtue. He should never forget that the ultimate end of life is *death*. And the meaning of virtue is immortality. The meaning of spiritual gain is immortality. Life is false—life is an illusion. Death is true—death is definite. Listen to some verses of *The Holy Bible, The Old Testament, The Book of Job, Chapter 14: Man that is born of a woman is of few days, and full of trouble. He cometh forth like a flower, and is cut down: he fleeth also as a shadow, and continueth not.*"

"Why does man commit evils?"

"Most of the men live in the Darkness of Ignorance and remain for away from the Divine Light.The world is full of the Darkness of Ignorance and most of the people live in this state of the world."

"Does God exist?"

"This is not a proper question. The proper question is whether man exists or not. Here I want to quote two lines from Alexander Pope's *An Essay on Man,* Book II: *Know them thyself, presume not God to scan; /The proper study of Mankind is Man.* Man fails to study himself. So he has no ability to scan God—to know God. God is a mystery for the ignorant people. Only that person can know God, who has spiritual vision—spiritual knowledge. Man should always choose the path of virtue."

"You say that man should follow the path of virtue but in this world of Ignorance it is not easy to follow it. There is evil everywhere in the world. None is safe in this world. In the past we were afraid of the wild animals but now we are afraid of man. Man is afraid of man. So, in such a critical situation it is not very easy to follow the path of virtue."

"The path of virtue should be followed at any cost. The man who follows it, he may suffer, but physically not spiritually. He must remember that the ultimate end of life is 'death.' There is no option of death. But death ends the life of the body not the life of the spirit. So man should follow spiritual path of advantage not the path of physical advantage. Physical loss is spiritual gain. The spiritual gain is the gain of the soul, which is immortal—which is true, but the physical gain is momentary—is false—is mortal. Man should prefer immortal gain. Death is a powerful agent which helps the body to change the physical form. So, death is the best friend of life. Evil is the enemy of life and virtue is the divine friend of life."

"What is wrong in this world?"

"Where there is no virtue."

"What's right?"

"Wherever there is the sense love, brotherhood, mercy, compassion, sympathy, tolerance, non-violence etc, is right."

"What's fate?"

"Fate is an unseen power which commands all mankind."

"Is there any role of duty in our life?"

"This is not a proper question. Man should do his duty honestly either he gains or loses. He should never think about the result of the duty done by him. Duty is commanded by fate...."

"Over all what is supreme for mankind?"

"Humanity is supreme. Man should remain far far away from the worldly evils; greed, lust, violence, intolerance, partiality, dishonesty..., as possible."

"What's the cause of my suffering?"

"Worldly evils have tempted you and you became the prey of the temptation as you lived in the Darkness of Ignorance where, there was no Divine Light. In lack of Divine Light man commits evils and suffers."

"Why did I live in the Darkness of Ignorance?"

"As you lack Divine Light."

"Why did I lack Divine Light?"

"Because of the worldly evils."

"My case is pending in the Supreme Court for hearing. I always think about it. What'll happen?"

"Don't think about all this. Perform your own duty honestly. God will help you. God will protect you. Nothing unwell will happen to you."

Meanwhile a messenger of the Supreme Court came and a letter was given to him.

Getting the letter he spoke, "... the next week is the most important week in my life. My fate will be decided very soon. I'll reap myself. I bleed. My house bleeds. My everything bleeds. There are the walls of thorns all around. None is with me. I'm alone. Now I know fully '*the sayings of the saints are nectarlike voices—are nectarlike fruits*'. But man avoids all this. Therefore, man suffers...."

"Nothing unwell will happen. God will protect you," said Swami Maharaj.

"I've committed a number of mistakes. I'm suffering from many diseases. I suffer. Only suffer. How will I be free from those sins?"

"Expiate yourself. God will pardon you. If you expiate, your sins will be gone—sins will be washed away."

"As I feel..., there is an important role of duty in man's life. Sin is following me. I think none will save me. None will protect me. The court will decide my fate, so...."

"Yes! Yes! Yes! Deeds follow man... go with death.

कर्मण्येवाधिकारस्ते मा फलेषु कदाचन। मा कर्मफलहेतुर्भूर्मा ते संङोऽस्त्वकर्मणि

Notes

i Bharatmata	:	mother India
ii Magahi	:	a regional language of Bihar, especially spoken in Patna and Magadh divisions.
1 chhathhi	:	a joyful celebration on sixth day of the birth of a baby (sometimes after more than six days).
2 dakshina	:	donation.
2 Sitaram	:	a Hindu name.
3 Ramayana	:	a holy book of Hindus composed by St Valmiki.
3 kothhi	:	palace.
4 paseri	:	An Indian measure of weight (paseries: plural number).
5 riyasat	:	estate.
6 Thakur Prasad	:	A publisher in Varanasi, Uttar Pradesh, that Publishes calendars, almanacs etc.
7 Brahmins	:	One of the highest or priestly castes among the Hindus. (singular number: Brahmin).
9 Mahabodhi	:	securing great knowledge.
9 bodhies	:	knowledge (singular number: bodhi).
9 Dushehra	:	Ashwin is the month when Navratri, a festival devoted to the Goddess

Durga is celebrated for nine days by Hindus and is celebrated as *Durga Puja* with gaiety and devotion. *Vijayadashmi* is celebrated on the tenth day. The tenth day is called *Dushehra* and is celebrated to commemorate the victory of Lord Rama over the Demon King Ravana. Giant effigies of Ravana are publicly burnt.

9 Deepawali : Deepawali is the festival of lights. It is celebrated on the Amawasya of Kartik, the eighth month of the Vikram Samvata. It is said in the Ramayana that Ram with his wife Sita and brother Lakshuman came back to Ayodhya after killing Ravana. The people of Ayodhya celebrated his victory and returning with thousands of lamps. Thus, the festival of Deepawali is celebrated by the Hindus. It is also known as Diwali.

9 Srikrishnajan-masthami : Lord Krishna was born at midnight of the Asthami in the month of Bhadra, the sixth month of the Vikram Samvata. Thus, it is celebrated at the time of night every year.

10 Shivaratri : Lord Shiva and Goddess Parvati were bound in the nuptial tie on troyodashi (13th) day of the first half of Falgun, the twelfth month of Vikram Samvata.

14 Ambassador : name of a car.

14 Marshal : name a jeep.

15 Baba : *i.e.* Hindu priest, mendicant.

15 namaskar bahinji : greetings to sisters, salutation to sisters.

20 Narad : a famous sage (here it means 'a person who creates quarrels').

22 Aqua-Guard : a water filter machine.

23 Guru gurúve bhawah	:	The preceptor is glory.
24 NSS	:	National Service Scheme.
24 Jayanthi	:	birthday.
30 water-fruit	:	a kind of fruit produced in pond.
33 gypsy	:	a kind of car.
35 McDowell's	:	*i.e.,* alcohol.
37 maidan	:	field.
40 falgun	:	twelfth month of the Vikram Samvata.
40 Lohia Maidan	:	name of a field named after the name of the great socialist leader Dr Ram Manohar Lohia.
41 Limcaman	:	*i.e.,* pen-name.
45 rajbhawan	:	office of the governor of the state.
46 Safari	:	a kind of dress.
55 faemalays	:	*i.e.,* meaningless word spoken only to stress the focus on the main word.
61 Granthis	:	religious priests of the Sikhs.
62 RCC	:	Regional Communist Centre.
65 faarm	:	firm
67 Lok Sabha	:	parliament.
67 Gandhi-cap	:	a kind of cap used by the political leaders of India.
68 dhoti and kurta	:	a kind of a traditional garment used by the Hindus.
68 Shriram Temple	:	a historical temple in Ayodhya, Uttar Pradesh at the birth place of Lord Rama.
68 Shrikrishna Temple	:	a historical temple in Mathura, Uttar Pradesh.
68 Baba Vishvanath Temple	:	a historical Temple in Banaras, Uttar Pradesh.
69 matribhumi	:	motherland.

Page	Term		Meaning
70	Lokpal	:	an officer to take necessary action against corrupt government employees.
70	company-raj	:	company rule.
71	panchayatiraj	:	local body rule.
73	deshdharma	:	patriotism.
73	sambidhandharma	:	to follow constitution.
73	Below Poverty Line	:	a standard to separate the poor to grant government facilities.
74	Hinduraj-Hindudesh	:	rule of Hindus for the country of Hindus.
74	Brahminraj	:	rule of Brahmins, the highest or priestly caste among the Hindus.
74	rajya	:	state.
75	malaidar	:	creamy.
75	rasdar	:	juicy.
75	mansal	:	fleshy.
80	AIR	:	All India Radio.
80	TV	:	television.
80	balbrahmchari	:	a celibate by birth.
80	lota	:	a kind of water pot.
81	balti	:	bucket.
81	rashtra	:	country.
81	kush	:	a kind of grass.
82	swadeshi	:	home made.
83	baboos	:	clerks.
87	bharat bhagya bidhata	:	determiner of the fate of India.
89	dukh-dard	:	miseries and sorrows.
90	rojgar guarantee scheme	:	employment guarantee scheme of the government in rural areas.
90	Jawahar Rojgar Yojna	:	an employment scheme of the government in rural areas.

90 Pradhanmantri Chaturbhuj Sadak Yojna	:	a scheme to built four-lane roads in India.
91 Boforce	:	a scam in which some political leaders as well as some... were allegedly involved.
91 Hawallah	:	a scam in which some political leaders... were allegedly involved.
91 Telecommunication	:	a scam in which some political leaders and officers were allegedly involved.
91 Fertilizer	:	a scam in which some political leaders... were allegedly involved.
91 MP-Quota	:	a scam in which some political leaders and officers were involved; this came to light after the sting operation by the private TV channel.
91 Bribe for asking question in the parliament	:	some members of the parliament took bribes for in the parliament asking question in the parliament. This scam waved the then Indian politics.
91 Coffin	:	a scam in which some political leaders... were allegedly involved.
91 Tantasi	:	a scam in which some political leaders...were allegedly involved. It was said that the land had been sold by the government at a very cheap rate.
91 Flood	:	a scam in which some political leaders...were allegedly involved and millions of rupees were defalcated by them.
91 Tehalka	:	a sting operation by a private TV channel, which allegedly showed corruption in Indian politics.
91 St Keats	:	a scam in which some political leaders... were allegedly involved.
95 forruption	:	*i.e.,* meaningless word spoken only to stress the focus on the main word.

95 batta	:	a meaningless word.
99 bohini	:	the beginning of sale in a shop.
100 panditji	:	a regardful word for the priest of the temple, a regardful word for Brahmins.
100 Saheb	:	a regardful word for the officers in India.
VVIP	:	very very important person.
103 dews	:	dues.
104 Super Post	:	a kind of mail to send a letter.
107 Bolero	:	a jeep.
109 Abhi Tak	:	a private TV channel.
113 doodh ka doodh; pani ka pani	:	an ideal justice, a justice based on facts.
115 trade	:	business of taking bribes.
118 haay	:	alas!
118 murdabad	:	short live, a slogan against any person.
120 Gandhism	:	Gandhian philosophy.
126 MacMahon Darra	:	name of a line.
127 Inqlab	:	revolution.
127 Jindabad	:	long live.
127 Gokhale	:	Gopal Krishna Gokhale(1866-1915), a Chitpavan Brahmin from Maharastra, a typical Congress Moderate leader.
127 Tilak	:	Bal Gangadhar Tilak (1856-1920), a Chitpavan Brahmin from Maharastra, Teacher, Journalist and Fearless Freedom Fighter; he is famous for his slogan: homerule is my birthright and I shall have it.
127 Gandhi	:	Mohandas Karamchand Gandhi (Mahatma Gandhi) (1869-1948); apostle of Peace and Non-violence;

		stellar role in Indian Freedom Struggle; remembered as Father of Nation.
127 Bose	:	Subhas Chandra Bose (1897-1945?); Kayastha from Bengal; resigned ICS 1920; President, Indian National Congress 1938, 1939, escaped to Germany,1942;Organizer Indian National Army, 1943, popularly known as Netaji.
127 Abul Kalam	:	Maulana Abul Kalam Azad (1888-1958); Born at Mecca of Indo-Arabian descent; eminent freedom fighter; Congress President; Education Minister in Nehru's cabinet.
127 Bhagat	:	Sardar Bhagat Singh (1907-1931); a fearless freedom fighter.
127 Azad	:	Chandrashekhar Azad (1906-1931); a fearless freedom fighter.
131 gandhists	:	Who follows the philosophy of Gandhi.
135 majars	:	tombs, graves.
135 Sufi	:	tradition of the saints in Medieval Age to abolish evils in Islam.
135 guru	:	preceptor.
135 ashram	:	institute.
135 peepal	:	a kind of tree.
136 Ashram Sandesh	:	name of a magazine.
140 कर्मण्येवाधिकारस्ते मा फलेषु कदाचन। मा कर्मफलहेतुर्भूर्मा ते संङोऽस्त्वकर्मणि।।	:	(Lord Krishna has said to Arjuna in the Bhagavad-Gita in Chapter[22], verse no: 47) Everyone's right is to work only. One shouldn't hope to get the fruit of one's work. Let not the fruit of action be one's object, nor let one's attachment be to inaction.

Index

A

Akashraj, 68
Almighty God, 6
Ambassadors, 11
Ambedkar, B R., 61
Ashram Sandesh, 121
Assembly election, 30-37

B

Baba Vishvanath Temple in Kashi, 62
Balbrahmachari, 72, 110
Bharat bhagya bidhata, 78
Bharatmata, 102
Bhitta, 76
Bose, Subhas Chandra, 61
Brahmins, 67
Buddhism, 53

C

Casteism, 1
Central Government, 50, 52
Chhathhi, 1
China, 114
Christianity, 53
Civil Code of Conduct, 56
Communism, 1
Coronation of the Limcaman, 38-47
Corruption-forruption, 85

D

Das, Jatin, 61
Dashrath, 4
Democracy, 49
Deshdharma, 65
Deshraj, 45, 85
Development Council, 22
Donation Collection Movement, 10
Durga Puja, 12

E

Election Commission, 38
Election for only stability, 60-69
Election, 96-103
End of the Corruption Movement, 22
Enemy of Corruption, 71

G

Gandhi Jayanthi, 28
Gandhi, Mahatma, 61, 107
Gandhism, 109
Gokhale, GK, 61

Granthis, 55
Guinness Book, 71
Guru, 120

H

High Level Commission, 83
Hinduism, 53
Hinduraj-Hindudesh, 66
Holy Quran, 54
Home ministry and red light men, 70-75
Honourable High Court, 25
Humanism, 54

I

Indian Railway, 81
Indira Awas Yojana, 81
Intermediate of Arts Examination, 9
Islam, 53

J

Jainism, 53
Jananayake Mubarakpur Samman, 37
Jawahar Rojgar Yojna, 81

K

Kamraj, 86
Kapilmuni, 5
Kashmir, 62
Kuber, 86
Kunda Estate, 4

L

Law in supreme in democracy, 116-119
Liberalization, 61
Lohia Maidan, 33
Lok Sabha, 60
Lokpal. 63

M

Mahabodhi of Sitaram, 10
Maharaj, Swami, 121
Majors, 120
Mercy, 24
Ministry of Disaster Management, 68
Model University, 9
Mother Tongue, 72
Mubarakpur Assembly Constituency, 30
Munda, Krishna, 77

N

Namaskar Bahinji, 15
Narad, 20
National Assessment And Accreditation Council, 23
National Front, 61
National Security Council, 40
Nehru, J L, 61
New Welfare Party, 47

O

OBC, 74

P

Pakistan, 62
Panchayatiraj, 63
Paseries, 4
Pillage and the A+ university, 25-29
Pradhanmantri Chaturbhuj Sadak Yojna, 81

R

Racialism, 1
Rama, 1
Ramayana, 3
Ram-Rajya, 62
Religion for scandal, 53-59
Right to information, 48-52
Robbery, 1

S

Sadhna, 117
Safari, 41
Sahib, 92
Samadhan Commission, 104
Samadhan commission, 83-95
Samibidhandharma, 65
Saturn, 120
Schedule Castes, 63, 74
Schedule Tribes, 63
Shamin, 117
Shriram Temple in Ayodhya, 62
Sikh, 53
Singh, Bhagat, 61
Sitaram and his realization, 120-125
Sitaram, 18
Special Commission, 102
ST, 74
State Information Commission, 51, 52
Student Union Election, 15
Sufi, 120
Swadeshi movement, 73
Swrod on corruption, 104-115

T

Thapar, Romila, 19
Tilak, B G, 61
Top secret meeting, 76-82

U

United Front, 61
USA, 64

V

Veer Sena, 56

W

Welfare Party, 38
Works of welfare, 18-24
World Bank, 64
Birth and happiness, 1-8
Achievement, 9-17